Micead Mwaxxle

THE SULIVANS
AND THE SLAVE TRADE

The record of a naval family from the War of American Independence to the beginning of the twentieth century, and in particular of Admiral George Lydiard Sulivan and his part in the fight against the slave trade.

Admiral George Lydiard Sulivan

THE SULIVANS
AND THE SLAVE TRADE

Peter Collister

REX COLLINGS LONDON 1980

First printed in Great Britain by
Rex Collings Ltd. 6 Paddington Street
London W.1

© P. Collister 1979

ISBN   086036 121 7

Typeset by Malvern Typesetting Services Ltd
Printed in Great Britain by The Pitman Press, Bath

CONTENTS

ACKNOWLEDGMENTS

I am most indebted to Major D. L. S. Hodson, grandson of Admiral George Lydiard Sulivan, for access to letters, diaries, photographs and family papers; to Mr D. C. Simpson, Librarian of the Royal Commonwealth Society, who not only introduced me to these sources of material, but has been an informed and friendly critic; and to Colonel J. A. Sulivan, great grandson of Admiral Sir Bartholomew Sulivan, who gave me access to his family tree and other useful information.

INTRODUCTION

Although the central figure of this story is Admiral George Lydiard Sulivan, he cannot be considered in isolation from his family, its long naval connection and the individual members, especially his elder brother, Admiral Sir Bartholomew Sulivan. The tradition of seamanship was such that he could scarcely have failed to be a good seaman, and the inheritance of an uncompromising religious faith was so strong that his reactions to the slave trade were almost predestined. When he spoke out against its evils and the legal restrictions inhibiting the Navy's efforts, it was as if his grandfather who had abhorred the trade in North Africa, his kindly father, his pious mother and his warm hearted brother as well as the cousins who served in West and East African waters were all speaking through him. For this reason I have chosen to call this book, which is both more and less than a biography, '*The Sulivans and the Slave Trade.*'

In the first chapter I have tried to fill in the background of this nautical family whose tradition continued into this century (George Sulivan's nephews were Commander James Sulivan, the first Briton to be born on the Falkland Islands, Lieutenant Thomas and Captain Harold Sulivan; and his great-nephews were Captain John and Vice-Admiral Norton Allan Sulivan, who died in 1964).

In the second chapter, I have attempted to depict the Naval background and to describe the origins of the slave trade in East Africa before dealing with his first voyage to those waters.

The third chapter concerns the exploits of both brothers in the Crimean War and as this was the only great European war in which they took part I have had no hesitation in including it despite its apparent irrelevance to the slave trade for it was to have a lasting effect on both of them.

From Chapter 4 onwards, George takes over almost completely—and so, for that matter, does the slave trade.

I hope this book, however inadequate, will rescue him from obscurity, although his name has long been respected by those who have read about the comparatively little-known war against the East African slave trade. I hope that the reader will come to appreciate his qualities, to bear with his weaknesses and to remember that he was a man of his time, not of ours.

LIST OF ILLUSTRATIONS

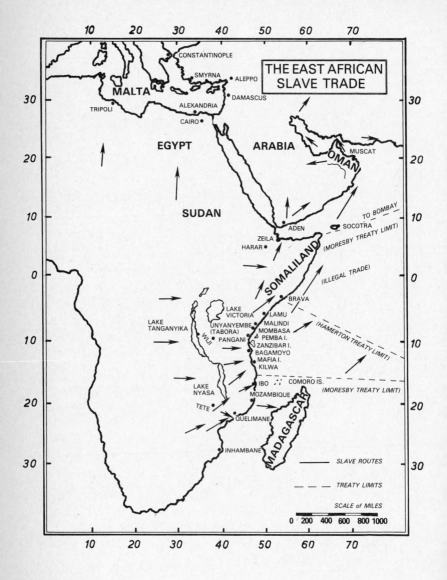

THE EAST AFRICAN
SLAVE TRADE

CONSTANTINOPLE
SMYRNA
ALEPPO
MALTA
ALEXANDRIA
DAMASCUS
TRIPOLI
CAIRO

EGYPT
ARABIA
OMAN
MUSCAT

SUDAN

TO BOMBAY
ADEN
SOCOTRA
(MORESBY TREATY LIMIT)
ZEILA
HARAR

(ILLEGAL TRADE)
SOMALILAND

BRAVA
LAKE
VICTORIA
LAMU
(HAMERTON TREATY LIMIT)
LAKE
TANGANYIKA
UNYANYEMBE
(TABORA)
MALINDI
MOMBASA
PEMBA I.
WIJI
PANGANI
ZANZIBAR I.
BAGAMOYO
MAFIA I.
KILWA

IBO
COMORO IS.
(MORESBY TREATY LIMIT)
LAKE
NYASA
MOZAMBIQUE
TETE

MADAGASCAR
QUELIMANE

INHAMBANE
———— SLAVE ROUTES

- - - - TREATY LIMITS

SCALE of MILES
0 200 400 600 800 1000

CHAPTER 1
A SEAFARING FAMILY

On the twenty-eighth day of December 1752, half way
between the fish and the flesh markets in the port of
Falmouth, was born to Joan James, daughter of a Cornish
farmer and wife of an eccentric retired naval officer, her
ninth child, Bartholomew, whose apprenticeship to the sea
began at the age of eleven with a voyage to Madeira and the
West Indies. In 1776, at the age of twenty-four he was master
of the fifth rate* *Orpheus* in Boston harbour when the rebel
batteries ashore opened fire on all British vessels and subsequently served ashore with skirmishing parties. On one
occasion, as he was wearing a white linen coat similar to
those worn by the colonists, he was taken prisoner by a
ferocious group of Hessians (German mercenaries recruited
in Hesse) who only reluctantly let him go. He had already
encountered their Teutonic methods of warfare when earlier
in the day he had seen one of them 'sever a rebel's head from
his body and clap it on a pole.'

His first command was the tender *Dolphin*, an old tub
with 'grass on her bottom a foot long,' which proved incapable of evading a line of ships led by an 'English' frigate
which turned out to be French, a fairly common occurrence
in eighteenth and early nineteenth century naval operations,
when ships captured from the other side were taken into use,
often retaining their names. After submission to a French
boarding party and imprisonment on St Domingo, he was
delighted to find on return to Jamaica, that he had obtained
his commission as Lieutenant as well as receiving a £300
share in prize money.

Bartholomew James was now 'as happy a fellow as ever

*See (p 26) viz. rating system for ships in H.M. Navy.

crossed salt water.' He joined the sloop *Porcupine* in time to take part in the capture of Omoa on 17 October 1779, and after a brief leave in Cornwall he was at the landing at Hampton Creek in Virginia, and on 2 April 1781 helped to capture a rebel privateer of fourteen guns and seventy men, loaded with rum and indigo, which he sailed with a prize crew to New York where he found himself in charge of a party who commenced a very thorough press, rounding up unwilling recruits for His Majesty's Navy. For the next fifty years this was to be a bone of contention between the young Republic and the British Navy and there were many men who served in the navies of both countries.

The press gang under Lieutenant James was 'furnished with droll yet distressing scenes,' such as 'taking the husband from the arms of his wife in bed,' but they were soon exchanged for more honourable enterprises when *Chevron*'s lower deck guns were landed for the defence of Gloucester and York, followed by a period of constant detached duty ashore and afloat including the command of a fire ship that 'ran two French ships of the line ashore.'

At the siege of Yorktown *Chevron* was set on fire with red hot shot but James was once again with the guns in front of the army when the enemy were repulsed, in spite of the Hessians breaking line. 'I want words to express the dreadful situation of the garrison,' he wrote, describing the 'noise and thundering of the cannon and the distressing cries of the wounded.' A shell burst between him and another Lieutenant, resulting only in contusion of his face and right leg. On 19 October 1781 the military garrison surrendered to the Americans and the Navy to the French. The French naval officers were 'very civil' and protected their English captives from the predatory clutches of the Americans, and shortly afterwards the British naval officers were sent home, spared the long drawn out hardships of their military comrades.

After the 'only idle three months' of his life, James was appointed second-in-command of the cruiser *Aurora* and was at Spithead on 30 August 1782 when *The Royal George* sank with Admiral Kempenfelt and 'eight hundred of the brave.' He was in command of *Aurora*'s boats which managed to rescue some of the survivors. After a few more adventurous episodes with pirates in the Channel and the capture of a smuggler laden 'with gin and tea,' *Aurora* was paid off in 1783 at the end of the war and James found himself in Falmouth, a half-pay Lieutenant. He engaged in a number of commercial enterprises and his financial stock became low. He was not a man given to self-criticism, and he ascribed this state to the failings of others. He commanded a merchantman in which he had a part share and sailed her to the West Indies and America, where he was equipped for privateering.

In 1794, at the start of hostilities with France, his ship, *Maria*, was taken over as a government transport and he found himself appointed as one of twelve Fleet agents, performing to a large extent the duties that in later years would be undertaken by paymasters and supply officers.

In Barbados attendance to 'mustering, victualling, watering, and in every aspect regulating such a number of transports full of troops, baggage, provisions and ammunition kept them from morning to night on duty.' On 3 February 1794, they sailed out of the harbour to 'the bands of music, the sounds of trumpets, drums and fifes.' With heart-felt relief, he contrasted this scene with the impecunious preceding years and blessed the absence of the bailiffs, lawyers and constables who had so plagued him on land: 'I go to pursue again the profession I was bred to, no longer within your diabolical reach,' he wrote of his creditors.

James helped with the landing of stores at Martinique where the troops made an opposed landing, but he became increasingly dissatisfied with this role, for 'to be an agent of transports was to be looked upon as an officer who had no kind of pretention or claim whatever to honour and glory.' He therefore volunteered to command a detachment of seamen and once more found himself serving on land as a soldier until the French surrendered.

Not long after this he was with the besieged garrison in Fort Matilde, Guadaloupe, where his room in the barracks was blown up by underground mines and he only managed to save his clothes and his grog. The French blockade tightened and James was 'at the batteries day and night.' On 19 November, when the naval landing party was withdrawn, he wrote 'the seamen as well as myself felt unhappy in taking leave of the General and the whole garrison with whom for thirty-seven days we had fought . . . never having taken off our clothes except "to shift" and that very seldom, nor slept on anything for most of the time but a hard plank at our quarters.'

He sailed for home, leaving the West Indies where, he wrote, 'my life was in jeopardy every hour,' but once back in Falmouth, he found even greater dangers awaiting him from his creditors. On the morning of the day that his wife and other ladies were to dine aboard, he was shopping in Portsmouth market when he was accosted just as he was buying asparagus by 'two savage bailiffs' who marched him off and secured him in a lock-up house at Portsea. There he gave his last half-guinea to a fellow naval officer whose ship was due to sail that very night and who needed only that amount to repay his debt. This imprisonment proved to be a blessing in disguise (though he was niggardly in his appreciation) for that night *Boyne* caught fire and went up in flames; 'the guns went off and she blew up and disappeared in an instant,' fortunately with no ladies dining aboard for this merry party had been cancelled because of James's imprisonment. *Boyne* took to the bottom with her all his clothes, chests, books and instruments.

After service on *Commerce de Marseilles* as First Lieutenant and another brush with the bailiffs of Portsmouth, he joined *Victory* in the Mediterranean as her Lieutenant.

Admiral Jervis had moved his flag to *Victory* and James joined her in 1796 shortly before his forty-third birthday, in time to take part in the long drawn out blockade of Toulon, spending a total of nine months at sea without once quitting station or anchoring, being victualled by transports from Corsica. Then on the very day that he was promoted Master he was attacked by virulent gout, which so incapacitated him that he found himself ashore and savouring the attractions of

Corsica with mixed pleasure and his usual critical petulance. 'How kind has Providence been to this dirty indolent race of mortals,' he writes of the inhabitants of the island. At Naples he called on the Hamiltons and paid his respects to Prince Frederick Augustus, sixth son of the Sovereign, then staying in the Neapolitan kingdom, and was overjoyed when the Prince accepted his hospitality. He did not think any more of Naples than he had of Corsica and particularly disliked the Neapolitans' 'indecent brutish custom of making every corner of the street a conveniency.'

However, he was not to be left for long fulminating on the ways of foreigners. As acting Captain of a prize vessel *Mignonne*, he searched for a French privateer in the Adriatic, and as Captain of the sloop *Peterel*, he sailed to Corfu where he was made much of and presented with enormous keys for two boxes at the Opera House.

A captain arrived from England to take command of *Peterel*, and James found himself unemployed on the island of Elba. On 21 December 1796, his forty-fourth birthday, he gave a dinner for Commodore Nelson, the captains of the squadron and several field officers of the army. Shortly after this he took command of *Dromedary* , a sixth-rate, whose previous captain had been dismissed his ship and four of whose officers were facing a court martial, and was with this unhappy ship in Lisbon when the British fleet at last met the Spaniards, missing the great battle of Cape St Vincent. As he was not yet a post-captain he had to be content with temporary commands of which the next was the *El Corso* brig, which had eighteen six-pounders and a crew of one hundred and twenty-one men. En route to Tenerife they were sighted and pursued by nine enemy ships. The Spanish ships ran up their flags in confidence of a prize and steadily gained on the little brig. Great seas washed over her as she tore along under every possible stitch of canvas; twenty water casks were stove in and thirty-one pigs of iron ballast were thrown over in order to lighten her, but still the Spaniards gained, opening fire with their bowchasers. Shot was splashing into the water all round and ahead of *El Corso* whose anchors were cut away. The crew threw overboard everything they could lay hands on: beef, pork, rice, vinegar and flour all went over the side in a final attempt to elude a capture which now seemed inevitable. The officers slipped below to pack their effects and seamen pulled on all their spare clothing. A Spanish seventy-four came ploughing through the stiff seas, her bow wave all foam, until she was within hailing distance, and in desperation the crew of *El Corso* now threw over the gun carriages and guns, for there was no thought of fighting, only of evasion. Just then, sudden heavy gusts of wind blew up accompanied by rain, and James ordered the brig to reduce sail, to put the helm aweather and to bear up out of the way of the Spaniards, a sudden manoeuvre executed rapidly before the squall developed its full force that put the Spanish into total confusion, running on into the storm whilst *El Corso* made good her escape. As all the officers except James were under twenty-four and none had looked forward to incarceration and loss of prospects any more than he had done in the West Indies, Captain James now came in for a good deal of admiration and gratitude, and they continued their cruise in good heart although they only had two guns left.

Once again and for the last time, Bartholomew James took part in shore operations: on this occasion he was in charge of the seamen at the landing at Grand Canary. Returning to Cadiz, he was reinforced by a motley crew of men of all nations including six former mutineers, for this was the year of the great mutinies at the Nore and Spithead and there was dissatisfaction in some of the ships of the Mediterranean fleet. Of his new crew he wrote, 'though I had great reason to dread my people who were men of all nations and many delegated from the Channel fleet . . . I gave them no time for reflection . . . good wholesome victuals, constant employ and very severe flogging for every offence was their allowance.' There were further actions off Tenerife and privateers were chased, one flying American colours. At Carthage he amused himself 'rowing into Tunis harbour more with thoughts of Dido and the Trojans than I did about two French vessels.' He arranged an appointment with the Bey, who kept him waiting so long that James returned to his

Admiral Sir Bartholomew Sulivan

Woodlands

HMS *London*

Ships crew of HMS *Daphne*: Central seated figure Captain
Sulivan

Freed Slaves on HMS *Daphne*: photograph taken by Captain
Sulivan

Cartoon from scrapbook of Sir Bartholomew Sulivan showing George on the point of being presented to Queen Victoria suddenly recognizing his brother Bartholomew in the queue behind him and turning his back on Her Majesty to greet him.

boat and was about to be rowed back to the ship, when a party of horsemen arrived with a carriage to transport him back to the Palace. The Bey blamed the charms of his seraglio for this omission, and asked James to point out the persons who had initially refused him entry. Two men were bound and would instantly have been strangled had it not been for James's intercession on their behalf. In Tunis he was sickened by the sight of slavery and the trade in slaves which his grandson was to abhor.

He sailed back to Gibraltar, meeting the convoy of captured French ships taken by Nelson at the Battle of the Nile, another great fleet action that he had missed. On Sunday, he was reading Divine Service and had 'just reached that incomparable prayer of the sea service wherein we solicit relief from the dangers of the sea and the violence of the enemy,' when the officer of the watch whispered to him that four Spanish frigates were bearing down on them, and they could see the crew of the leading frigate preparing boats' parties for boarding. Once again, officers and men began packing their gear preparatory to imprisonment, but once again James put his ship about so rapidly that they escaped this fate.

Soon after, he obtained his long awaited promotion to Post Captain and took command, first of *Canopus*, eighty-four guns, and then of *Franklin*, one of the French ships captured at the Nile.

He retired as a Captain in 1799 and bought himself a house called Woodlands near the quay at Falmouth. Here, no longer plagued by his creditors, he and his wife Henrietta (*née* Pender, herself belonging to a family of sailors) could dispense a hospitality whose warmth was enhanced by the memory of the years of privation. One of their daughters, Eliza, married a sailor—Captain Vaillant of the Dutch Navy, and on Christmas Day 1807, the other daughter, Henrietta, first caught the eye of her future husband, Commander Thomas Ball Sulivan.

Sulivan's father, Timothy, had been born in 1754, only two years after Henrietta's father, and was a man cast in the same salty mould—patriarchs of a family that was to follow

the sea for another two hundred years, including amongst
their direct descendants at least fifteen known naval officers
excluding the many naval men who married the daughters
and grand-daughters. According to Timothy Sulivan, he was
the senior member of the line of Timothy O'Sullivan of
Clonfert and should by rights have inherited the title of
O'Sullivan More—or Chief of the Sullivans—of which the
last holder had died in 1746.* (At the end of the nineteenth
century, Athlone Pursuivant of Arms held this to be a
reasonable claim, although disputed by the branch of the
family who spelt their name with two L's.) The fly-leaf of his
Bible showed him to have been born on 14 September 1754,
naval records give his birthplace as Cork, and the family
tradition was that he had run away to sea. He was certainly
pressed off a merchant ship in Bristol in 1776 and obtained
his warrant as a gunner in 1787. He fought at St Lucia in
1778, Granada in 1779, under Hood against de Grasse and at
the Chesapeake in 1781 and at Saintes in 1782. There must
have been occasions when he was serving in close proximity
to Lieutenant James in North American waters; perhaps the
founding fathers of this seafaring family may even have met
or served in the same ship. In 1782 he was one of the prize
crew of *Caesar* when she blew up, and subsequently was not
only wrecked in *Centaur* but was one of eleven survivors who
crossed the Atlantic in an open boat. He was also in *Neptune*
at Trafalgar and was still serving in her as Master Gunner
when he died on 20 March 1808 and was buried at sea.
Timothy Sulivan and his wife Elizabeth (*neé* Bryan) had
eight children of whom Thomas Ball Sulivan was the eldest.
He had been First Lieutenant of the brig that led Nelson's
fleet through the Baltic and had served in *Anson* at the
capture of Avacão, but at this time, in 1807, he was on half-
pay and unemployed and had gone for a channel cruise as
guest of his old Captain, Lydiard, in his old ship, *Anson*. In
Falmouth harbour on Christmas morning they were told that
all Captains were expected to dine with the James's, and on

*His grandson George was to reactivate this claim during his retirement.
(Chapter VII.)

protesting that they knew them not, were informed that this was immaterial and that the James's would take it ill if any senior naval officers were not to dine with them. It was a festive party and Sulivan left it determined to renew acquaintance with Miss Henrietta James. This he did a few days later, under the saddest of circumstances.

Anson sailed on Boxing Day for her station on the western part of the Channel and on 27 December was in Mount's Bay trying to battle her way against a southerly gale. She could make no headway and anchored off the eastern shore of the bay. Suddenly two cables parted and it became clear that the remaining ones would not hold her, in which event she would have been dashed against the rocks with the loss of all on board. Captain Lydiard consulted his officers and they decided to try and run the ship ashore on the sands of the cove before dark. The plan was successful, but there were still terrible hazards. As soon as she struck the seas threw her broadside on, and all the officers and men who had congregated on the poop, thinking it to be the safest place, were swept off by great pounding seas. The masts went at the same time but by good fortune the main mast fell in such a position as to form a bridge from ship to shore, so that the men aboard had only to observe carefully the waves at bow and stern and then, judging the right moment, run to shore along the mast. First over were six women, followed by most of the crew. Meanwhile, Captain Lydiard and Commander Sulivan had lashed themselves to the stanchion of the wheel and from this point of vantage they heard the surgeon's young son, who had accompanied his father, call out, 'What would Mama say if she knew of our position now?' Both father and son were lashed to the gun tackles on the weather side of the ship and at that moment a great sea hurled the young midshipman right across the ship between two guns with such great force that it killed him outright. The surgeon let go his own lashings and tried to cross the deck to his son's assistance, but the next sea dashed him also against the lee side, killing him instantly. At length, when everyone else appeared to have left the ship, Captain Lydiard said, 'Sulivan, it is our turn now. You go first.' They watched the receding seas and ran from the wheel to the mainmast, when they saw a boy clinging to the gear round the stump. Sulivan, seeing a wave coming, dropped cross-legged on the mast, clinging to the ropes for dear life, but when he turned round, all he could see was an empty deck where the boy and his captain had been a minute before. He ran across the mast to the beach where he was told by those ashore that Captain Lydiard had been trying to help the boy when the wave struck.

News of this disaster was brought post haste to Woodlands where James was celebrating his birthday with a dinner party whose guest list reads like a roll of honour of the Royal Navy: Nelson, Parker, Saumarez, Pellew, Cockburn, Freemantle, Macnamara, Coffin and Hamilton were all there when the news was brought. All had experienced the furies of the elements and knew how much greater these hazards were than dangers from the enemy.

Thomas Sulivan was brought back to Woodlands and made much of, and not long after, he married Henrietta. He continued to have an adventurous career, commanding *Woolwich* on the expedition that took naval crews to man the lake flotillas in Canada in 1809, was wrecked on the island of Bermuda, captured a French frigate in 1814 and took part in the actions off the Chesapeake and the expedition against New Orleans in the American War of 1812, before retiring to Falmouth in 1815.

Meanwhile, his father-in-law was still going strong. During the height of the Napoleonic invasion scare, he commanded the Cornish Sea Fencibles and stumped round the coastline with all his old vigour, retaining command until 1814. At the Jubilee of George III he gave a dinner to the poor of the neighbourhood, including a two hundred pound sea pie, which, according to the *Royal Cornwall Gazette*, made the 'hearts of the poor people sing with joy.' He was promoted Rear-Admiral on the retired list and took a great interest, not only in his son-in-law, who also became a Rear-Admiral on the retired list, but also in Sulivan's three brothers, Sam, James and Daniel, who had all served in North America and two of them at Trafalgar; they all retired as Lieutenants and, much to the annoyance of West Country yachtsmen, proceeded to win all the regattas in their large Causand Bay boat, *Sweet Poll*. At last, full of years and honour, and in modest comfort, the old man died in 1828.

The Sulivans were a prolific family, for Thomas Ball even outdid his father Timothy by having twelve children of whom nine predeceased him, and when he was buried in his family vault at Mylor churchyard there were already nine inscriptions ranging from Norton Sulivan who lived for one year to Lieutenant Norton Sulivan who died at the age of thirty. After the service, as he left the graveside the family doctor, Dr Miller, said 'there lies the best husband, the best father, the best friend.'

The three children who survived were Commander Thomas Digby Sulivan who died in 1876, Admiral Sir Bartholomew James Sulivan and Admiral George Lydiard Sulivan, named after his father's old friend, the Captain of *Anson*. Little is known of the first and of the last much more will be said. The second of them, Bartholomew, married into an interesting naval family, for his wife Sophia was the grand-daughter of Admiral James Young who was Admiral of the White. He had had two wives, each of whom gave him a son. Both sons also became Admirals: Sir William Young, GCB., Vice-Admiral of England (notorious for his rapacity over prize money when Port Admiral at Plymouth), and Admiral James Young by his second wife. This James Young married Charlotte Fryers, daughter of Lieutenant-General Fryers, RE, who served fifty-six years in the army and died Deputy Commander-in-Chief in Ireland in 1829. When in Gibraltar he designed the famous garrison library where his portrait by Hoppner still hangs.

The formative influences that shaped the character of George Sulivan were: the sea tradition of both sides of his family, in particular the exploits of Grandfather James, the upright nature of his father, the piety of his mother and the example of his elder brother to whom he was very close. Indeed, Bartholomew was to have such a profound effect on his younger brother that neither can be considered in isolation. He was born at Tregew in the parish of Mylor beside Falmouth harbour on 18 November 1810, and was despatched at the early age of twelve years and three months to the Royal Naval College, Portsmouth, a fairly recent establishment to which there was still considerable antipathy in the service. Neither Bartholomew's father, Rear-Admiral Thomas Ball Sulivan, nor his grandfather, Rear-Admiral Bartholomew James, had had much formal schooling, naval or otherwise, for the sea service had been one in which boys were quite literally apprenticed to their trade, be they ship's boys or midshipmen. Nevertheless, even though he attended this new-fangled academy where he studied English, geography, history, mathematics, French, fencing and dancing, in addition to spending much of his time in the rigging loft, Bartholomew still had a difficult ladder to climb.

His first appointment was to *Thetis*, whose crew were known to the rest of the Navy as 'The Tea Chests' because their ship had been selected as a test case for an experimental reduction of the rum issue from half to a quarter of a pint.

Thetis, a fifth rate commanded by Sir John Phillimore, sailed in the spring of 1825, and after a minor confrontation with Spaniards at Gibraltar, left for Rio de Janeiro. The 'Collegians' (as the Naval College midshipmen were called) received no academic schooling aboard, but Captain Phillimore saw to it that their seamanship was not neglected and they had plenty of training aloft. Every afternoon the officer of the watch assembled the midshipmen and put them through their paces. First they had to take in the lighter sails such as the flying royal and the mizzen top gallant studding sail, then they had to do an exercise like taking in a reef in the topsail and hoisting it; almost immediately they would have to lower it again, take in a second reef, hoist, lower once more, form a third reef, up again and shake it out. It was this sort of training, day after day, that made young midshipmen into seamen.

In South America *Thetis* acquired a new Captain, Bingham, who addressed the ship's company with these words: 'You shall have every indulgence the service can allow, but there are three things I never forgive; drunkenness, disobedience, insolence. Pipe down.' A model of clarity.

This first voyage was followed by another to South America where Brazil and Argentina were now at war, and on one occasion when Bartholomew Sulivan and some fellow officers were out riding on hired horses they were fired on by a troop of cavalry. At sea also they had some experience of war when they were fired on by an Argentinian squadron commanded by an Englishman, Admiral Brown, many of whose crews were English and American sailors.

On 15 December 1828 Sulivan joined the surveying sloop, *Beagle* as midshipman under Commander Fitzroy whom he had known as First Lieutenant of *Thetis*. This was only a brief appointment and was followed by two years in *Ganges* and *North Star* before, having passed his Lieutenant's examination, he once again joined *Beagle* and sailed to South America. *Beagle*'s task was to survey the coast of South America in order to complete a chain of meridian distances round the world. As well as starting a lifelong interest in marine surveying, Sulivan also developed his interest in botany and sent home plants to the botanist Lindley. Even Darwin noted his correctness in observing scientific phenomena. His main work, however, was as surveyor and this entailed a high standard of seamanship, for it was all done under sail in two survey boats purchased and fitted out by Fitzroy at his own expense. In twelve months they surveyed from the River Plate to the Straits of Magellan in conditions of great hardship, often soaked to the skin. They were, in fact, very similar conditions to those which his younger brother George Lydiard, who was born during this period, was to experience nineteen years later off the East African coast.

On Christmas morning 1834, Bartholomew Sulivan and his boat's crew went foraging on a small island inhabited only by Indians and, despite a downpour of rain, they managed to acquire some eggs for a plum duff and a sheep, and by four o'clock they had 'one side of a sheep roasted, another side boiled, 12lbs. of English fresh roast beef heated (he does not explain how this came to be fresh) and two immense plum puddings . . . and . . . in spite of two-thirds of the party being West Countrymen we had enough for supper also.' His last survey voyage was to the Galapagos Islands in the yawl before rejoining *Beagle* for her journey home *via* New Zealand, Sidney, Mauritius and the Cape. She arrived at Greenwich in November 1836 where she excited great interest and was visited by many people.

In his memoirs, Sulivan hardly mentioned Darwin, but admired Fitzroy; as he made no reference to the latter's celebrated quarrel with Darwin, it is reasonable to assume that his relations with the scientist were not close. Certainly he and his brother were both convinced Christians in an age when conformity and conviction were not necessarily synonymous. This was due to their mother's training. She had been brought up in modest luxury at Woodlands during the only affluent period of Admiral James' life. Later, much of his estate, derived from prize money, was lost through misplaced confidence and generosity and the James's had to leave Woodlands. She was a cultivated woman who had studied music and made her sons learn poetry for which they were afterwards grateful. Bartholomew used to repeat the poems by heart in the long night watches. She brought up a family of four children on very small means, sustained by pride, faith and a sense of humour. She had made her husband promise to read one of the appointed psalms daily and to say the collect for the Sunday Communion Service, and just before his death he said that he had never omitted the prayer and very rarely the psalm.

Between the years 1842 and 1846, Bartholomew took part in the Parana Campaign in South America. The young Argentine Republic that had emerged from the war of independence against the Spanish was ruled by President de Rosas, who, after securing power in Buenos Aires, had to deal with opposition in the Banda Ovental province and its capital Montevideo whose inhabitants were encouraged to resist by hopes of British support, although the blockading fleet was commanded by an Englishman, Admiral Brown, in the pay of de Rosas. Paradoxically, the town's desperate defence was assisted by another Englishman, 'Cockney

Sam,' who raised a force of soldiers, mostly Basques and Piedmontese, whose red shirts, in imitation of the redcoats of British regiments, were subsequently taken over by Garibaldi who had also raised a force in South American waters composed mainly of Italian seamen from coasting vessels. Britain and France had guaranteed the independence of Banda Ovental (Uruguay), and when Rosas attempted to gain possession of both banks of the River Plate, they were forced to intervene. When he refused to withdraw, Brown's squadron was captured and British and French squadrons ordered to re-open the Parana, the great river that flows into the Plate.

Meanwhile, Bartholomew Sulivan in *Philomel* had been continuing his painstaking survey work. For two years there was not a single entry in the ship's punishment book, such was the basis of trust by which he exercised leadership over his men. His wife and her three children were in Montevideo, the only English family who had not fled. As befitted the daughter of Admiral Young she was a woman of great courage and calm and even accepted with equanimity the crashing of a cannon ball into the front of her house, for de Rosas's General Oribe was at that time encamped only two miles in front of the town and Brown was still blockading by sea.

In August 1845, the combined French and British fleets began operations on the coast of Uruguay, and had it not been for Sulivan's charts of these waters they would have been in great difficulties. In company with *Ganges*, *Dolphin* and *Fanny*, *Philomel* sailed up the Uruguay river that runs roughly parallel and to the east of the Parana, and were joined at the Rio Negro by the 'Buenos Ayrean' squadron under Garibaldi—'a regular mosquito fleet of twenty, from a sixteen gun brig to whale boats, little more than a party of buccaneers' as Sulivan described the heterogeneous force. *Philomel* sailed in the van, constantly taking soundings. In November the combined squadron sailed up the Parana river, after the sailors had been hurriedly drilled for the shore fighting that was expected. Here the French had the edge on the English, for all French sailors at this time were trained to fight as soldiers. By the night of 18 November, they had almost reached the port of Obligado, guarded by a battery and a chain stretched across the river. That night Sulivan and a French officer each set off in a small boat, the crews rowing with muffled oars, and each took soundings close up to the chain. Sulivan was in command of the left division with *Fanny* and the French ships *Procide* and *Expeditive*, the right division being composed of the heavier ships in order to be more abreast of the batteries. The plan was for the left division to go first to give covering fire, and on the morning of 20 November in fog, with a light breeze, they set sail. Moving very slowly in the light airs they saw the guns of the batteries pointing towards them; as they were making laborious headway against the stream, the enemy opened fire. Sulivan wrote afterwards, 'I had just been forward to fire a shell with the starboard bow gun to try the range—and then had gone aft to look to the steering when I saw a crash on the forecastle. A huge shot flew past my head.' In this initial encounter, the fore topmast was cut half through and the main topsail came down when the tie was shot away. Soon the whole deck was covered with splinters of wood and iron. The other vessels of the left division were suffering similar experiences as they anchored and fired their broadsides, despite being swept back by the strength of the tide.

Meanwhile the right division was labouring up slowly, making hard work of it as the wind had now dropped to very light airs. *Dolphin* had nineteen men killed or wounded and all the vessels came under fire. They all had difficulty in taking station and with dragging their anchors. In particular the French *San Martin*, which was left unsupported in an exposed station, suffered terribly, being struck by thirty-six round shot, yet—as Sulivan emphasizes in italics—'she held her station.' The French steamer *Fulton* got up to the chain, being relatively untroubled by the great difficulties experienced by the other vessels—all sail; the airs were so light that they could not reach their stations and came under heavy and accurate fire. Sulivan even feared for a time that they would be unsuccessful, but the crew of the one anchored enemy vessel that had done considerable damage to the French and English ships, deserted her and by midday also several of the guns had been silenced. Up in the batteries the enemy were commanded by old Admiral Brown's son, clearly visible in a white waistcoat; the guns were commanded by an American named Thom and the gunners also included American and British sailors amongst their number. The chains were cut with three sets of saws, used by volunteers who came under heavy fire, and *Fulton*, *Firebrand* and *Ganges* sailed through followed by the armed boats' parties, Sulivan amongst them accompanied by a young cousin (later Captain W. Sulivan). They landed so close under the batteries, fortunately, that many of the guns could not depress low enough. Sulivan personally spiked five of them under heavy musketry fire which killed his coxswain. The action was now virtually over. The French had had fifteen men killed and forty-five wounded, the English nine killed and twenty-seven wounded. Sulivan was congratulated for his part in the action by Captain Hotham and, although glad to have accounted himself well, wrote later:

It is dreadful to think of the carnage . . . there are above a hundred dead bodies, all most dreadfully cut to pieces by round shot . . . every day we have found poor wounded wretches alive . . . English, Americans, Spaniards, Russians etc., and a number of poor blacks. I trust I may never again have to enact a part in such a scene and yet I am astonished with myself and rather disgusted at my want of feeling, that the second day I found myself moving among these bodies as unconcerned as if they were not human beings and examining the effects of our shot, yet when I thought how many my own hand might have put to death, it certainly made me shudder. . .

The ships slowly ascended the Parana river towards Rosario, meeting no further resistance except from the current and a hostile plague of mosquitoes, until they reached San Lorenzo. Writing of this period and of a proposed attack with insufficient men, Sulivan wrote, 'my own mind is made up not to care for what people may say or think; but if I am sent on service and have reason to think that . . . the losses are likely to be more than the thing is worth, I will not attempt it.' They reached Goya where they found an encampment of Paraguayan troops, for Paraguay was also at war with Rosas who refused to acknowledge its independence, and Sulivan's comments are interesting: 'Dr. Francia, the dictator, not only shut up Paraguay, but by a system of terror also shut up the ideas and minds of all the inhabitants . . . it is interesting to observe what the effect of being brought up under such a system has on the character of the people.' As *Gorgon* had been left in an exposed position three hundred miles below Corrientes, Sulivan volunteered to take her down to the Squadron at Santa Fé and to bring up the smaller steamers newly arrived from England. Accompanied only by two boys, he steered her down river—'the most anxious work I ever had'—through very narrow channels with numerous lakes and a three or four knot stream. He returned up river with *Dolphin* and *Fanny*, and once again came under fire at the cliffs of San Lorenzo when the enemy batteries galloped up to the cliff, shoved their muzzles over the top, fired and galloped back again. He returned to Corrientes as a passenger in the steamer *Alecto*, newly arrived from England, where she aroused great interest, 'hundreds of ladies coming and going.' By now, the province had been saved, for the Paraguayan General Paz, after several defeats, had at last repelled the invaders, and they returned down river once again coming under fire at San Lorenzo. On arrival at Montevideo, they learnt that a revolution had taken place within the government party, and as urgent despatches of this news had to be sent to London, *Philomel* was chosen to take them; she sailed for Falmouth, was paid off at Plymouth and Sulivan was summoned to London to give Lord Palmerston information.

He was now a Post Captain, and after serving as Colonel and Chief of Staff of the Royal Dockland Volunteer Brigade (shades of old Admiral James and the Sea Fencibles) he spent a further eight-and-a-half years on half-pay (as Nelson and many others had done during periods of limited activity and few commands). During this time he took three years' leave

of absence to go to the Falkland Islands which he had surveyed some years before. He sailed in a chartered vessel
accompanied by his wife (to whom he had given less than a
fortnight's notice, and who was shortly to give birth to
Henry Norton Sulivan), his friend Captain Philip Ham-
mond, his five children (of whom the eldest was then eleven),
a governess, a manservant, a maid (who very soon married
one of the queue of Falkland bachelors), a piano, some
animals and a young stallion—Hastings—whose descendants
can still be found on the islands. In 1851 he left for home,
unfortunately missing the arrival of a letter that might have
enabled him to save the lives of Captain Allan Gade, RN,
and his companions who died of starvation on Tierra Del
Fuego where they had gone with an inadequately equipped
expedition for missionary work. Later, Sulivan was a
moving spirit in the revival of the mission and helped to raise
money to fit out a mission schooner and a headquarters on
the Falkland Islands. He remained an adviser to the South
American Mission Society to the end of his life. Years later
his son wrote of him:

> My father showed his faith by his work. It was said of
> him that his entrance into the messroom did more to stop
> any objectionable conversation than the appearance of the
> chaplain. He showed great interest in the moral and
> religious welfare of the men under him. A strict sab-
> batarian, he avoided all possible work on Sunday. He
> would never accept an invitation to dinner on that day
> even from his Commander-in-Chief, and would rarely
> write a letter home. There being no chaplain in such small
> vessels as he commanded, he not only conducted the
> ordinary services himself but instituted classes as well.
> When duty called he exposed himself fearlessly to danger
> with the fullest knowledge of the risk he ran, but with a
> simple faith in a Divine Providence watching over him.

CHAPTER 2

ASHORE AND AFLOAT

In 1832, two years after Bartholomew and his boat's crew
had eaten their Christmas dinner on an island the other side
of the world, his younger brother George was born at
Bridgend Cottage, Mylor. Ten other children had been born
after Bartholomew and one was still to come. After selling
Woodlands in 1809, Grandfather Bartholomew James had
lived with his daughter and son-in-law, Thomas Ball Sulivan,
at Tregew and then at Mylor, and had been dead only four
years when George was born. He grew up in a house full of
the memories and mementos of the old man and of the Navy
of the eighteenth century.

Although some of his older brothers and sisters were
christened in Church, possibly for expediency, George was
baptized at home by the Reverend Timothy Wildlove of the
Independent Chapel, and remained a dissenter all his life,
like his mother Henrietta, who wrote during his earliest days
in the Navy:

> I hope you will have a nice place of worship. If there is an
> Independent Chapel go sometimes. You were baptised in it
> and it is the Church of your parents and fondly loved
> sisters, but go to Church too if you like. Never be ashamed
> to own that church in which your mother received truest
> blessings, in which your sisters grew up to be shining
> lights. There are many in the Establishment but they may
> take charge of churches and thousands of souls without a
> spark of grace. Never blame or condemn what others
> think. Never say one word against the Church of England
> but if anyone blames you for being a Dissenter firmly
> declare your attachment to it and say as little as you can.

Life at Bridgend Cottage could hardly have been luxurious

for the second youngest of a family of twelve whose father had refused honours through his inability to pay for them, but George grew up with a deep love for his home and its surroundings.

Falmouth was then one of the busiest ports in the kingdom, being the most westerly and one of the largest and safest of English harbours. The entrance was more than a mile wide and there was deep water even at low tide. A *Panorama of Falmouth*, published five years before George Sulivan was born, gave details of thirty-eight Packets with regular sailings to ports in the West Indies, Mediterranean, Brazil, Cartagena, North and South America and Mexico. It also contained a description of the harbour with '400 sail of merchant vessels of various description and ten or twelve ships of war' . . . of the population, of whom 'in the last census of 1821 there were 957 houses, 1840 families' . . . and of the town, 'full a mile in length . . . and its very excellent enclosed market with a fountain of pure spring water at the centre.' The main industries were the Pilchard Fishery, tin and copper mines. Timber for the mines and for building was imported and so was 'sailcloth, hemp, tar, hides, sugar cotton, wines.'

There were four hotels and twelve inns, 'the whole of which afford comfortable accommodation for Naval and Commercial Gentlemen.' There was a Consul from the United States and Vice Consuls from twelve countries, including Russia and Brazil, as well as from the States of Hamburg, Lubeck, Bremen and Oldenburg. Altogether it was a striving, bustling seafaring community with boats, sailors and ships very much in evidence, so that a young boy growing up in a naval family would be surrounded on all sides by the evidence of the sea.

Contemporary paintings* of Falmouth Harbour depict a serene anchorage sheltered by friendly hills, with just a hint of rough seas beyond, with ships of all sizes at anchor and under sail.

The parish of Mylor, in which Sulivan was born was

*J. M. W. Turner, 1826

described shortly after his death by Hugh P. Oliver in *Notes on the Parish of Mylor 1907*, as abounding 'in most delightful views, which are presented to the eye in every direction . . . On the south side from the grounds of Trefusis it commands a view of the magnificent harbour of Falmouth, enlivened by the shipping of all nations . . . Lofty elms surround the churchyard which also contains two specimens of yew, these are very ancient and cast their shadows far and wide over the tombs of parishioners whose remains rest beneath their branches . . .'

Amongst these graves were those of the Sulivans, later to include George Sulivan's mother and father, and all his brothers and sisters except Bartholomew. Nine of them predeceased their parents and died before the age of thirty-two.

George Sulivan left the security of home to join the Navy as a cadet in June 1846—the year that saw the repeal of the Corn Laws and the beginning of the end of the old squirearchy. Britain was already the first industrial nation of the world. The dark satanic mills had spread like a stain across her northern hills and there were stirrings of conscience. The great Reform Bill, passed just before Sulivan's birth, had altered the composition of Parliament, and there were new men from a new industrial society. The new railways, now in their boom period, tarmacadam roads, a recently introduced postal service, were bringing people closer together. Two years later Europe was to be torn by revolution in most of her major capitals, and in England the Chartist riots were to engage the attention of the aged Duke of Wellington. The army had not significantly altered since he had commanded it at Waterloo in 1815 and he had for years kept a tight control over reform. The Navy, however, had changed in two important respects since the time of George Sulivan's grandfathers. The 1760s, when each began his service, was a period of intermittent warfare that lasted with few breaks until 1815, and during all this time the great problem was the manning of ships. The modern division between a merchant service and a fighting service was not accepted, and the nation's ships and seamen were regarded as a bank which could be drawn on in times of crisis and left largely to its own devices at other times. Hence the custom of hire and discharge, whereby the crews of naval ships were paid off at the end of each voyage. Only for officers was there a permanent professional *cadre* and even they were only retained on half-pay during periods of peace or when there was no command available.

The only answer to the manning problem of the eighteenth and nineteenth centuries had been impressment. In the year 1801 there were over three hundred thousand men in the armed forces out of a total population of over fifteen million, but in 1851—five years after George Sulivan had joined the Navy—there were only just over two hundred and ten thousand out of a population that had grown to over twenty seven million. Thus, the great burden of how to man the ships that had so beset the naval authorities from Pepys's time onwards, whose scars of impressment and mutiny had left such a mark on Nelson's Navy, had been lifted. In this respect, therefore, George Sulivan's navy had radically changed from that of his father.

The muster book of *Victory* for 16 October 1805, five days before Trafalgar, shows that out of a complement of eight hundred and thirty six, not less than three hundred and nineteen were pressed. Much, therefore, had depended on the quality of the officers and it was in this respect that the navy differed from the army. For the naval officer social divisions as between one ship and another were nothing like as great as those between cavalry and infantry, and expensive regiments and others; nor could he purchase his way into rank and regiment with few duties beyond an occasional guard mounting. He went to sea as a boy and family influence extended only as far as the need to have a seafaring relation to whom to be attached until he became a midshipman. Even this had its value as it confined the Service to a large extent to those families with nautical connections. The naval officer had to learn his trade the hard way; he took his turn aloft and on watch, he learned to navigate, and he imbibed sea lore so that he became a true professional. On the whole, naval officers came from modest backgrounds, mostly from the south and west country squirearchy, from parsonages and rectories, such as Nelson's, or from the seashore homes of nautical ancestors, as in the case of George Sulivan.

The normal routine of a man-of-war in the first half of the nineteenth century when the Sulivan brothers were both serving, differed little in essence from the great days of Nelson at the turn of the century. The seamen were woken at four or five in the morning to the noise of boatswains' pipes and shouted commands, decks were holystoned and washed down, guns cleaned and hammocks stowed before breakfast was piped at eight. The crew were divided into four divisions each under a lieutenant who was responsible for the general welfare of the men under him. In addition, each man belonged to one of two, occasionally three, watches—the starboard and the larboard (port) watches. Each sailor was ranked as able seaman, ordinary seaman or landsman—this last going out of use sometime after the end of the Napoleonic wars. At any given hour of the day there would be one watch on duty and the other off. This comprised the whole of the crew except for officers, warrant officers, petty officers, servants, and tradesmen such as the sailmaker, ropemaker, baker, tailor and so on. In addition to the regular work of each watch, when men would be required to go aloft to man the yards and work the sails, as well as to pull and haul in the waist of the ship, there was also a regular routine of training at gun drill, cutlass and musket drill, reefing and furling sails, and manning guns at target practice. Thursdays were usually 'make and mend' days in peacetime. Orders were kept to a minimum on a well regulated ship and were obeyed in silence, each man knowing his own place and function. When the ship's company was summoned to 'action stations,' by drums beating the rhythm of 'Hearts of Oak', the men would assemble at their stations, boarding parties would stand by with cutlasses and pikes, others with swab and buckets, powder monkeys with powder, every man knowing his job and his place.

This meticulous order and precision which was the hallmark of the fighting ship was achieved by strict discipline. A ship remained at sea for many months on end, its complement composed largely of uneducated, illiterate men, who were not even issued with uniforms until 1857, and discipline was essential. Under a just and good Captain like Nelson, punishments were used but as a deterrent, and sparingly, and the Captain's sincere interest in his men's welfare was so patent to all that the men would obey anything for his sake. Nevertheless, even in the mid-nineteenth century discipline could be severe if the letter of the law were to be obeyed. Life below deck, even in the mid-Victorian navy was a hard one, and as late as 1847, the year after George Sulivan joined, there were eight hundred and sixty floggings, usually administered by the master-at-arms or the corporals.

Discipline was only relaxed when a ship came into harbour, and even in 1822 Admiral Hawkins, an evangelical naval officer wrote of the boatloads of prostitutes that met every warship in port, who descended to the lower deck with the men who picked them out, where, 'each man being allowed only fourteen inches breadth for his hammock . . . they must be witnesses of each others' actions . . .'

The seamen did not have much to spend upon their pleasures, naval pay always lagging behind that of the army, and wages were often paid in arrears, one of the difficulties being that before the introduction of paper money a ship's company could only be paid in hard coin on her return to a home port for paying-off. Men were therefore often not paid for years after foreign service. The Commissioners would come on board and each man received his pay, after numerous deductions, inside his hat, with the amount chalked on the brim. A few days ashore with the ladies of the town and the pay—such as it was—would be gone. No wonder that prize money loomed so large and so long in naval thinking. Innumerable Prize Acts were passed throughout the eighteenth century, but the crux remained that the value of any prize taken went to the crew concerned, according to rank.

The Navy in which the Sulivans served in the eighteenth

century and the early years of the nineteenth was a hard service. Money was poor, conditions spartan, but there were compensations. One was grog, issued twice a day, at noon and at six in the evening—steadily reduced in strength throughout the century—and the other was the substantial quantity of food compared with what agricultural or urban workers could obtain ashore. In 1805, for instance, a seaman would have a pound of pork on Sunday, two pounds of beef on Tuesday, another pound of pork on Thursday, and another two of beef on Saturday. He had butter and cheese three days a week, a pound of biscuits every day as well as two gills of rum and a gallon of beer.

The ships on which the seafaring Sulivans served throughout the eighteenth century differed only in degree of size and speed and sail area from those of their predecessors in the seventeenth century, when the system of rating, still in force during Sulivan's service, was first instituted. It was during the reign of Charles I that naval ships were divided into six 'rates', with further sub-divisions of classes. The prime object of this was to determine the rates of pay of the officers and seamen, which varied from class to class, based on the number and dispositions of the guns carried. The majority of ships of the line were third rates, two deckers with seventy-four guns. First and second rates, usually flag ships, carried upwards of ninety guns. The most numerous of ships 'below the line' were fourth and fifth rates, carrying twenty-eight to thirty-eight guns on a single deck, known during the eighteenth century as 'frigates'; these acted as the 'eyes of the fleet,' as 'repeating ships' for signals, carrying urgent despatches, protecting trade and harassing the enemy merchant shipping. The smallest rated ships, sixth rates, carrying twenty to twenty-four guns, were the smallest type of ship commanded by post-captains. Similar French ships were known as '*corvettes*,' a name subsequently introduced into the British Navy.

Below the sixth rates were a number of 'unrated' classes, of which the largest were sloops, mounting fourteen to eighteen guns, originally with a particular type of fore-and-aft-rig, but later including square-rigged vessels known as ship-sloops and brig-sloops. Below these were gun-brigs and cutters, and a miscellany of types such as bombs, fireships, gun-boats, surveying ships and yachts.

The year before George Sulivan joined his first ship, the Admiralty had ordered a number of iron frigates. There were already steam vessels in the Navy list, but mostly fulfilling fairly humble functions. The great men-of-war were still full-rigged sailing ships. But now, with the introduction not only of steam but also of the screw propeller to supersede the clumsy paddle, and the plentiful supply of iron, more suitable as a hull for the new stresses resultant on the use of engines, the Navy began to change its shape at the time that Sulivan joined. The iron frigates became troop ships after a public outcry at this interference with the 'wooden walls,' and in the Crimean War there were indeed a few small steamships, but not iron ones, and the fleet consisted still of sail of the line, a few only with engines as afterthought. Towards the end of the war, the French, who were always ahead of the British in technical innovation in the nineteenth century, produced the new element of armour plating and their wooden steamers, covered in two-inch iron plates, were very successful. Inevitably there was a chain reaction to this, particularly the development of rifled breech-loading gun barrels projecting cylindrical rotating shells. In 1860, the frigate *Warrior* was built of iron throughout and fully engined with screw propulsion. Thereafter all capital ships were built of iron until replaced by steel in the 1880s. Nevertheless, *Warrior* and her successors continued to be fully-rigged sailing ships until, in the seventies, the first sail-less capital ship, *Devastation*, was built.

When George Sulivan joined the Navy, he was to serve in a service whose outward form had changed comparatively little since Trafalgar and whose ships were still recognizably the same breed that Nelson had known. In the year after his death, 1905, the great *Dreadnought* was built, fundamentally the same species as the battleships of the World Wars of the twentieth century. But Sulivan, whose life and service spanned these changes, was to spend most of his days under sail or in ships that were primarily sailing vessels.

At the age of fourteen, deeply imbued with naval lore, young George left his family and home in the first of innumerable partings. When he wrote to say he was homesick, his mother answered: 'Your future welfare depends on rising above thinking so much of home while your present getting forward will make you so much happier in a year or two.'

His first ship was *Spartan*, in which he served in home waters from 1846 to 1848. He settled down happily enough, for his mother wrote:

> It is a comfort you like your ship . . . As it is your temporary home be as snug and happy as any place away can be although it is being away makes home so precious . . . Bear and forbear and get on safe with your superior officers and if it is in your power get in the good opinion of your Captain . . . but all must be by first seeking the helping hand of God to hold you . . . Cast every fear on Him and cheerfully perform your duty . . . Avoid drinking, gaming, swearing, profaning the Sabbath by amusements on that day. Whatever work you may do in the way of duty by command of others is not profaning it . . . but to devote a part of that day to pleasure by your own inclination is sinful . . . My dear child, you are seldom out of my thoughts, what a comfort writing is.

As the wife, daughter and granddaughter of sailors, she knew something of the temptations of the life when she warned him to 'acquire the power over yourself (through prayer and dependence on God) to enable you to rise above the slavery of extravagance. Never take more than enough to do you good. When you find yourself unusually exhilarated in spirits, very bright, be sure you have gone beyond the proper bounds.'

He was posted to *Castor*, and his mother wrote, 'You could not be going away under more favourable circumstances, a good climate, a nice ship and lots of comforts to take with you.' In 1849 he sailed for the Cape and wrote home from Tenerife a letter which his mother said 'gave us all so much pleasure,' and in August he saw, for the first of many times, the majestic hump of Table Mountain rising above the bay. *Castor*'s Captain, Wyvil, was also Commodore of the Cape of Good Hope and East Coast of Africa as far as the fourth parallel of southern latitudes, and young Midshipman Sulivan was to spend a large part of the next eighteen months detached in boats' crews off the East African coast in an attempt to combat the slave trade.

The indigenous people of East Africa consisted of many different tribes, while along the coastal belt Arabs and Persians had established a cosmopolitan Islamic civilization of petty Sultanates and city states, flourishing at the time of the Middle Ages in Europe. The first contact with Europe had come when the Portuguese superimposed a loose overlordship over the Sultanates between the fifteenth and eighteenth centuries, distinguished by frequent revolts, especially by the people of Mombasa where they had built their immense fortress of Fort Jesus. The Portuguese were driven southwards by the Omani Arabs under Seyyid Sa'id, who moved his court in 1840 from Oman to Zanzibar, which had now become the centre of an Arab empire. After his death in 1856, the empire was divided into two, the Sultans of Zanzibar ruling only the island and exercising suzerainty over the coastal Sultanates, whilst Oman retained a separate identity. Zanzibar continued to be the centre of the slave trade conducted to a large extent by Arabs from Oman, whose dhows transported the slaves captured by wealthy Arab slavers in the regions of the great lakes and marched to the coast in long caravans.

The first stages in the protracted struggle to end this trade had begun in 1822, when the Moresby Treaty was signed by Captain Fairfax Moresby RN, and Seyyid Sa'id, who agreed to forbid the sale of slaves to Christians and to limit the trade by forbidding ships from his dominions to sail south of Delgado or east of a line from Dieuhead to near Socotra. In 1839 the forbidden area was further increased and in 1845 the slave trade between Zanzibar and Oman was prohibited. Thus, legally, the only trade now permissible was between the towns of the East Coast and Zanzibar itself, but as Sulivan and his shipmates were soon to learn, this meant very little.

Castor was detained at the Cape because of a convict dispute in the colony, and her boats, consisting of a pinnace, barge and a private boat given to Captain Wyvil in Muscat on a previous tour of duty, were hoisted on board *Dee*, which arrived at Madagascar in October and at Angoche the following month. On the 15th the boats were hoisted out, manned and armed in preparation for exploring the river. No doubt young George Sulivan, at the age of seventeen, felt some tingling of anticipation that day, before he set out on detached boat duty, as his brother, father and grandfather had done. It was not unlike looking for a needle in a haystack, for the navy had so few ships for this work, and the slavers' intelligence network was so good. 'Slavery had not been abolished in the U.S.A., South America, Portugal or the Spanish settlements,' wrote Sulivan twenty-four years later of this period, 'therefore there was a large trade going on with these countries from the East coast of Africa. There was also a large trade with Brazil, especially from Quilimane, which actually increased after its independence as the Brazilians did not feel bound by international treaties and Cuba also imported twenty three to fifteen thousand slaves a year. These vessels, often disguised as whalers, 'would anchor at the entrance of a river and aided by dhows, in one night would take in cargoes of several hundred of slaves.'

Sulivan wrote feelingly of the great slave market at Mozambique, in Portuguese territory, as large as that of Zanzibar, both of them sources of a human 'Nile' which 'empties itself into the slave ocean of Persia, Arabia and Egypt.' The population was reduced at the rate of one hundred and eighty thousand a year, of whom only a third reached the coast. From the long seaboard of the East African possessions, ten thousand slaves a year were exported, and the economy of Mozambique was based on this trade. Portugal was nominally committed to ending it, but however sincere intentions were in Lisbon they were largely ignored by many local officials. Prophetically, Sulivan wrote 'the immense wealth of Africa which now lies buried and dormant is yet, I believe, destined to be brought to the surface when its trade will take the place of the present iniquitous slave trade . . .'

It was in the knowledge that the dice were heavily loaded against them, for there were so few men-of-war, and so many people were in collusion with the slavers, who had the sanction of a legal trade co-existing with an illegal one, that the young men set out on the morning of 16 November 1849 in the boats of *Castor* and *Dee*, and proceeded up the river Angoche (Sulivan called it 'Angoxa') towards the fortified town of the same name that had been attacked a few years before by Portuguese troops and boats' crews from *President* and *Eurydice*, who had been repulsed with heavy losses.

The little fleet consisted of *Castor*'s pinnace under Lieutenant Campbell, Midshipman George Sulivan and twenty men, with one twelve-pounder gun; the barge under Second Master Albert, with Midshipman Patterson, fifteen men and a three-pounder; *Dee*'s first paddle box boat under Second Master Jones, with a midshipman, eighteen men and an eighteen-pounder; the second paddle box boat under Master's Assistant Dye with eighteen men and an eighteen-pounder; the gig, under Lieutenant Crowder who commanded the expedition; and the cutter with Dr Evans. They proceeded up river in line and anchored for the night inside Monkey Island, where, after the awnings had been spread and the boats anchored close together, the mainbrace was spliced, with quinine mixed in the spirits, 'Sweethearts and Wives' were toasted, and each boat's crew sang a song in turn before turning in to lie under the awning, listening to the lapping of the water against the boat, the hum of mosquitoes, and the other myriad sounds of a tropical African night.

Early the next morning they continued up river and at one o'clock they rounded a bend and had their first view of the fort, with a vessel close hauled underneath it. As they approached, a red flag was hauled up, and the incessant beating of tom-toms continued to sound. At four o'clock, at short range, fire was opened on the boats from the stockade and two sailors were severely wounded, but they continued to advance, now in line abreast, under heavy fire, which they returned, with shell, grape and cannister. The tide was rising, and every now and then one of the boats would ground, for there was scarcely enough depth of water to get close to the stockade. Some of the Arabs were firing at *Dee*'s boats on the right of the line, from a large dhow of one-hundred tons, hauled close on the beach, and this gave the sailors the justification for attempting to destroy her, without prior inspection to ensure that she was a slaver. The fort was silenced mainly by the spherical case shot fired from Sulivan's boat that burst so accurately within the stockade that the Arabs were driven into a wood on the right from which they kept up a fusillade of musketry. Dye managed to get under the stern of the dhow, which he boarded and set alight, coming under heavy fire from the Arabs who emerged from the woods, wounding two sailors. At five-thirty, the flotilla withdrew, only just in time to prevent their being left high and dry by the receding tide, and they returned to their previous anchorage where the wounded were treated.

The island of Mafamala off the mouth of the river now became the flotilla's headquarters. About three-quarters of a mile long, covered with casuarina trees and thin grass, and surrounded by a coral reef, it was an ideal rendezvous with a good channel and anchorage. The encampment consisted of four tents for officers and men, one for provisions and stores, one for ammunition, and two tanks of water, and at the head of the beach, a blacksmith's forge and a carpenter's bench were set up under canvas. Here they indulged in a Robinson Crusoe life, and as always on detached duty, relations between officers and men became much closer than under more formal conditions. They collected oysters, swam several times a day, hauled in nets and salted fish in casks for visiting ships.

Whilst some stayed on the island, others left on detached duty, and on 23 March, Sulivan found himself once again in the pinnace, this time heading southwards.

Sailing along the coast during the night, with scarcely a ripple on the water and just enough wind to fill the sails . . . the starlight was so brilliant that every object was clearly visible as on a bright moonlight night in England. The low coast lay outstretched before us from north to south; the men were all asleep and the silence was only broken at intervals by the flapping of a sail or an extra ripple against the bows of the boat, caused by a 'cat's paw' of a breeze, but beyond and on that long extent of coast, only a mile or two from us, was one almost incessant sheet of lightning illuminating the distant hills and broad extent of sea with the brilliancy of daylight and bringing the outline of the whole country in full relief . . . The scene became familiar to us afterwards, losing much of the charm of novelty, but never shall I forget the first night when we remained under weigh and I watched that supernatural light with almost rapturous awe and in the absence of any accompanying noise of storm was reminded of the 'still small voice' in the sacred writings.

During this expedition they anchored at another small island where they erected tents with boat sails and awnings.

In January, the *Pantaloon* brig called at Mafamala and an invitation was sent couched in the following terms: 'The Governor and Officers of the Island request the pleasure of the company of Captain Parker and Officers *Pantaloon* at five o'clock!' The guests were received by a guard of honour and a band consisting of fifes and a tin pot. The banquet consisted of 'kettle soup, a variety of fish, kettle entrées, fowls, salt junk, pressed vegetables and yam with plum pudding 'à la lower deck and an ample supply of beer and rum' . . . reminiscent of that Christmas dinner eaten by brother Bartholomew and his boat's crew on a small island off the coast of South America fifteen years before, when even his stalwart West Countrymen could not finish the immense plum pudding. The evening ended with the usual toasts, 'the Queen' and 'Sweethearts and Wives,' but also included 'The Boat's Crew' and 'An end to Slavery.'

Early in February they left their idyllic island existence for Mozambique, where they were attached to *Dee*, leaving in company with her for the Portuguese settlement of Ibo which was to form the chief rendezvous for the boats whose orders were now to cruise to the northwards, about a hundred miles of coast, up to Cape Delgado. The islands to the north were less healthy than those to the south and from now on they would have no more headquarters ashore.

Lieutenant Campbell had now left in order to take charge of a Spanish prize captured by *Pantaloon*, with four hundred slaves aboard, but Sulivan instantly took to his new commander, Mr James, Second Master of *Dee*, and on 15 February they set forth for new adventures. As they cruised northwards, landing at coastal villages, they were always alert for treachery, especially when the welcome was ostentatiously friendly. They boarded several dhows but were unable to capture any, although certain they were slavers. This was partly due to their own ignorance, as they expected to see fittings such as shackles and planks, which would be found on an American or European slaver, and partly to the lack of an interpreter, so although convinced of the guilt of certain Arabs, they could obtain no legal proof. Only an interpreter could ask the essential questions in Swahili whose answers would show if an African was truly a slave or not, and if so, if he was a 'legal slave,' one that had been taken at a port within the Sultan's dominions and was being carried to another one. As well as illegal slave-running dhows, there were coasters trading in ivory, copal, hides, rice and corn, which took on a few slaves for transport within the Sultan's dominions, but without a legal licence.

'A common practice,' wrote Sulivan, 'exists among Arab passengers in these dhows to pay the *Nahoda* (skipper) for their voyage by bringing a slave with them from the shore, the proceeds of whose sale at a northern market yields the passage money; it is just some cases as this that have been made use of by some persons to prove that dhows have been captured with only domestic slaves on board'—domestic slavery was of course still quite legal anywhere within the Sultan's dominions, and customary everywhere on the east coast of Africa.

Knowing as I do from experience' [he wrote, twenty-four years after his first cruise in East African waters] 'what a few slaves on board a dhow really means . . .

ASHORE AND AFLOAT 35

knowing also what the term "domestic slaves" signifies on the East Coast, I can only regret that the question of the slave trade on the east coast of Africa has not earlier forced the attention of the British public, that its true chracter might be understood; and I cannot suppress a feeling of pride that our determined efforts at its suppression, although they have raised the ire of petty chiefs on the coast (who, being subjects of our Indian Empire, manage to obtain the sympathy and interference of the Indian authorities, by whom, through being misinformed, the matter was misjudged) have at last had the effect of bringing the whole subject before the world.

He went on to describe some of the Arabs' dodges; in particular the custom of most Arab dhows of taking on board at each port two or three fairly healthy looking slaves who could pass as members of the crew. Detection was impossible without interpreters who could read the ship's papers which gave the true complement. When the numbers built up to a hundred or more, twenty or thirty were represented as the crew, and the women slaves were dressed in Arab costume and called passengers. When boarded by a naval party, these pathetic creatures sat around the ship in such dumb silence that their condition was obvious. Consequently, 'legal traders,' of this kind, carried about a third of the slaves to the more northern markets. Without an interpreter, who could easily detect this ingenuous subterfuge? The Navy was impotent. 'We boarded sometimes two or three dhows in a day, and recollecting how full many of them were of Arabs and Negroes, I feel convinced that hundreds of slaves must have so run the gauntlet and passed us . . .'

Even when the use of interpreters was adopted, there were difficulties, for—as Sulivan pointed out—without sharing in prize money, they had insufficient cause to withstand bribery, and at least one was found to be giving false information in order to get the ship out of the way of a slave dhow in which he had a pecuniary interest.

On the morning of 15 March, Sulivan's crew had an exciting chase after a dhow. On boarding it they found—

twenty or thirty negroes pretending to be very busy accomplishing wonders in unstowing or stowing some cargo, rolling up sails, hauling taut ropes that ought not to be hauled taut; they had no doubt been frightened into this vigorous and deceptive action by the usual Arab story that "white men eat black man if he get him".

About twenty others were dressed up in Arab costume, with a few African women by their sides, 'who never before were so rolled up in cotton, lashed up like hammocks, with nothing but their eyes appearing, and half-a-dozen genuine Arab brutes, one of whom appeared to be "monarch of all he surveyed."' The sailors' concept of cross-questioning was to ask a number of simple questions very loudly in English; 'How do you do?' (Shaking hands with everyone who chose). 'Where you come?' 'Where you go?'—a wave of the hand to north or south was assumed to imply Zanzibar or Mozambique. The interrogation continued: 'What dem nigger der?' They point to the sails and make a motion with their hands like that of hoisting it. 'Oh, dem crew men.' 'Who dese?' Another wave of the hand from south to north and a good deal of jargon in which the words 'Mozambique' and 'Zanzibar' again occur. 'Oh! Suppose dem passengers?''Where am papers?' The dumb-show of writing usually led to the production of papers which were, of course, incomprehensible, and as there was no physical proof of slavery, the vessel had to be freed, leaving 'the astonished Arabs in ecstasies of delight; and by way of expressing their overflowing gratitude—and surprise too—at our not taking their vessel, they passed two or three fowls and several coconuts into the boat; a gift which boat-cruisers were not likely to refuse, seeing that we were on salt provisions, and what was worse at that time, preserved meats.'

There followed Sulivan's first taste of monsoon conditions, a force five wind increasing rapidly until the boat had to be kept under weigh, the island not affording enough shelter. Seas washed over the bows and flying deck—a temporary deck round the gunwale—and sail had to be shortened. For two days they were unable to light a fire and lived on pork and biscuit, and the wind reached force eight before it finally abated and allowed them to seek shelter under the lee of the Gariamino island. On that night, wet and miserably uncomfortable, Sulivan smoked his first pipe— and enjoyed it.

The next day they were given information of a three-masted vessel to the north, which turned out to be non-existent, the information having been given in order to get the navy out of the way. Slowly they were learning the hard way—Sulivan was storing up experience that was to be invaluable when he returned to the coast as a senior officer. This was a war in which the British began, not only with their hands tied behind their backs, because of the co-existence of legal and illegal trades and their own lack of any authority or control in the area, but in which they also fought as if they were blind, deaf, and dumb, with no knowledge either of the language or of the ways of the country. But they were to learn, and things would be different when Sulivan returned.

They were now experiencing monsoon conditions, alternating between fierce heat, and downpours so torrential that they 'found it necessary to jump overboard to keep dry' leaving only two men in the boat, when under weigh, with their clothes under a tarpaulin. After doing this ten or twelve times a day for a fortnight, they had to send the cutter back with several men suffering from fever and dysentery.

On 5 April, entering the Ruvuma river against a three-knot current, they met a squall which threw the boat on her beam end. It was fortunate that most of the ropes were weak and rotten and that the sheets were carried away. The main halyards were let go and the boat righted just in time, the weight of the provisions bringing her up again, with water almost up to the thwarts. Had she sunk, none of the crew could have been saved, for the shore was a mile off and the current running out.

On 19 April, after nearly seven months of cruising, they sighted *Castor* again, and, for the time being, returned to normal big ship routine, with some regret after the free existence in small boats tempered by the pleasure of getting enormous batches of mail. George had a number of letters from home; his mother had written on 21 January, 'By the time you return from your station you will be quite a man, no longer little George.' She hoped he would soon become a lieutenant through his own powers of leadership, for it was a rank 'attained by many who are not valued as a gentleman or officer.' 'When I get my desk before me, I fancy I am talking with you' she wrote in another letter, and in another, 'I think it is worse for the friends of sailors than themselves. They move from one place to another and the time moves apparently quicker but here it is the same from day to day . . . What a heart cheering thought to a weary worn traveller the hope that we shall never sin . . . What a meeting with those we loved on earth but in the presence of Jesus . . .'

Sometimes we hear of Papa, in his garden, fishing, 'mixing a crab for dinner'; of neighbours and relatives, of the churching of the girl who was to marry Norton Sulivan and who belonged to the Free Church of Scotland of which Mrs Sulivan approved; of George's sisters, particularly Henrietta who 'carries the linnet from place to place, in and out . . . All goes on in the same monotonous manner . . . it must be very dull for those who have had constant variety.' Perhaps she was thinking of Papa. Only occasionally are there glimpses of a larger world; 'the great mass of the French who went to Italy to support the Pope are beat . . .' but mostly they follow the same pattern, starting with what she called 'my sermons,' the term her children used for them, going straight on without pause or punctuation into the trivia of daily life and ending with concern for George's spiritual and physical welfare: 'I think a great deal about you in that place . . . I don't like your going up rivers after slaves although my trust for all things that concern my children is fixed on God . . .You talk about going ashore for some grub, remember how many accidents have happened from such folly . . .'

On 29 April, *Castor* anchored in Zanzibar harbour where the 'abominable water' soon caused dysentery to spread throughout the ship. 'The usual civilities' were exchanged, and the 'undeviating custom among the Arabs of giving and accepting presents gone through, the Commodore receiving a very handsome Arab horse from His Highness, which remained on board for nine months, until the ship returned to the Cape, by which time it could do everything but smoke a pipe, and it is not certain that in another month it would not have done that too, for there were many efforts on the part of the crew to teach it that accomplishment.'

In Zanzibar the officers were entertained to dinner by the Sultan. Shortly afterwards, when twenty or thirty bullocks, sheep and pigs had been taken aboard—essential for long voyages—*Castor* sailed southwards, and continued to cruise almost continuously for nine months, leaving the coast only once during that period to refit at Mauritius, and Sulivan wrote 'Never did British man-of-war, since the blockading days of the French war, enter a port needing repair more from truck to keelson.'

At that time there were rarely more than three cruisers off the east coast, stretching from the Cape up to the equator, and as the extent and nature of the trade was scarcely comprehended, being equated with the west coast trade of which the navy had considerable experience, it is little wonder that *Castor*'s efforts were so ineffectual. However, they had some exciting moments. At the town of Keonga, the ship's boats landed on the beach, after information had been received that the barracoons were full of slaves, and as the boats grounded some way out the sailors had to wade ashore, the tallest sailor carrying Captain Bruce, the leader of the party, a very small man, under his left arm! 'In this undignified position in front of everyone he was waving his sword, in his usual energetic manner, and in dangerous proximity to his coxwain's nose, exclaiming "Come on, come on my lads, skirmishers advance!"' The men doubled up a pathway through the mangroves until they met a solitary Arab who said there were no slaves in the barracoons and that the sailors were at liberty to burn them. This was done and the party withdrew, a classic example of the total lack of surprise, local intelligence, or subtlety that characterized some of these early expeditions before the navy acquired expertise and knowledge.

In one village, the inhabitants after previous friendliness to the boats' crew, seized two officers, lashed them to trees, and threatened them with execution, which was only stayed by handing over muskets and cloth. 'In consequence of this issue, the boats of *Castor, Orestes* and *Dart* (the frigate's tender) were manned and armed, and sent up to the village to attack and burn it down; they found the village deserted, but as a lesson to the natives in future, set fire to every hut, and what was more serious to them, for the huts can be built in a few days again, cut some of their coconut trees down, which take seven years, after being planted as young trees, to bear fruit. They seldom build the huts except where the trees are well grown . . .'

Castor's cruise achieved little, but at least one officer was to gain invaluable experience for later years. The ship's boats had destroyed two slave dhows—that was all—although the rigours of monotonous cruising, climate, bad water and short commons had contributed to a sick list numbering nearly half the ship's company. The *Pantaloon* and the *Orestes* fared better, having taken several American and Spanish ships, with slaves aboard. *Castor* arrived at the Cape on 5 February 1851, sixteen months after the boats' crews had left them for Mozambique.

Here, George joined the Naval Brigade at Buffalo Mouth for service in the Kaffir War. Boer farmers, impatient of British restraint had, since the early thirties, trekked northwards across the Orange and the Vaal rivers and had eventually been guaranteed their freedom by the British Government, reversing the expansionist policy of the previous years. It was less than twenty years since the Boers had trekked away from British rule, and in that time the young Republic had been reduced to such a state of fragmentation and disorder that the Imperial Government had been forced to intervene to protect British settlers, and land between the Orange and Vaal rivers had been annexed. The Boers themselves were hopelessly at odds with each other and the Transvaal state had been divided into three republics under irreconcilable leaders. Previous British policy, which had refused to accept sovereignty over Natal, had then been reversed, mainly as a direct outcome of successive 'Kaffir Wars.' After the murder of the Boer Piet Retief by Dingaan in 1837, and the onslaught of the Zulu Impis into Natal, Briton and Boer had combined to defend themselves, and the skill of Napier and his hundred soldiers, as a leaven amongst the settlers, won the day. Natal was annexed and the Cape colony was extended westwards to the Orange river estuary and eastwards to the Kei. The previous policy of retaining a buffer belt of indigenous people between British and Boers was abandoned. There were now a number of Bantu tribes within the area of Imperial rule, whilst for the time being the Zulus remained outside it, with others—the Matabele and the Mashona—well to the north. It was at this point that there was a change in policy. Just at the moment when the Boer States were at their weakest, the three Transvaal States were recognized as independent and two years later the Orange Free State was also accepted by the British Government. The situation therefore in 1851 was that the British, prompted by the high cost of South African administration and defence, and with a growing preoccupation with the Eastern question in Europe, were already in a mood for retrenchment when the Kaffir war broke out. This was the eighth in a series of conflicts with the Bantu tribes, to whom was applied the loose appellation of 'Kaffir.' The first of them had taken place in the seventeenth century when the Cape was still under the rule of the Dutch East India Company. Conflicts then had been between the Dutch and the Xosas, Tembus, Pondos, in the east, and the Hereros in the north, and subsequently between British forces, sometimes in loose alliance with Boers, against the same tribes. Later came the wars with the martial Zulus and the Basutos, and the augmentation of the small Imperial garrison by the locally recruited Cape Mounted Rifles and police force.

The month before *Castor* had arrived at the Cape Hottentots and Kaffirs had destroyed much of the country between Grahamstown and the Orange river, and many homesteads had been abandoned and herds of cattle driven off. General Somerset who had repulsed an assault on Fort Hare by Fingos, was hampered in his efforts by the indifference of those Dutch settlers away from the frontier area, by anti-war propaganda in Cape Town, active support for the Kaffirs by some missionaries, by lack of forces and by inadequate security of communication between Grahamstown and Williamstown. The troops at his command consisted of the 45th Regiment, the 74th Highlanders, veterans of Kaffir wars, Cape Mounted Rifles, native levies, and elements of gunners and sappers; and with this small force at his disposal, the Governor, Sir Harry Smith, had to deal both with the Kaffir invasion and the internal simmering revolt of the Dutch settlers. For the moment, however, the most formidable adversaries were the Kaffirs beyond the Fish river, fifteen to twenty thousand strong, as well as marauding bands of plunderers, all of whom were firmly based high up in the Amatola mountains. The only answer was to attack, to harry them in their own lairs and to drive off their cattle.

By the end of February, the force had swollen to nine thousand men, including three thousand regulars, and a small party of seamen and marines from *Castor*. A table of units and personnel engaged in the campaign lists seven 'subalterns,' five 'serjeants,' and one hundred and three 'rank-and-file,' from the Navy. In all probability Sulivan was one of the 'subalterns.'

Patrols were sent in strength to Fort White and Fort Cox, and in March the enemy were stormed on Mount Pegu. Conditions were very rough for the men; the country was baked hard and the heat intense: there was constant marching, skirmishing and ambushes, and once the advance started into the Amatolas the heat and sun gave way to rain and sleet and a bitter wind from the snow-capped mountains. Captain King of the 74th Highlanders described the advance to the foothills: 'The General, with his staff, appeared on the ground, where the whole division amounting to two thousand men, artillery, cavalry, infantry and irregulars, stood drawn up in column; the advance and rear guards were formed; and we moved off to the inspiriting air of 'Hieland Laddie' . . . The quick-step changed into the farewell melody of 'Auld Lang Syne' as the long, waving line of hardy sunburnt troops marched steadily past in column of sections . . . The pipes then struck up 'Over the Border' and played us across the frontier into Kaffir land, through the whole of which the pipes afterwards accompanied, inspiriting men on many a long and weary march . . .'

The forces made laborious progress through dense forest studded with enormous masses of detached rock, wildly overgrown, with tangled asparagus trees, endless monkey ropes and other creepers. Slowly they trudged through dense thorny undergrowth, concealing dangerous clefts and crevices and strewn with fallen trees in every stage of decay, while the hooked thorns of the 'Wait-a-bit' tree clung to their arms and legs, snatching the caps off their heads. The going was tough for the British soldiers, for although some had been issued with a grey canvas jacket in lieu of the useless and heavy coatee, they still wore heavy equipment (with leather pouches untanned to replace the peace time black), and most of them were armed with heavy muskets, though six men in each company had been issued with the first *minié* rifles, muzzle loaders firing a conical bullet.

Not only were there weary marches, but the fighting was hard and fierce. On one occasion the enemy allowed the Highlanders to come within range and then opened fire. '. . . for a quarter of an hour,' wrote Captain King, 'there was an incessant roar of musketry and whistling bullets. As we neared the top, scrambling with hands and knees up the crags, which we now discovered to be of enormous size, and in places unsurmountable, the fire became hotter, the balls striking the ground and sending the earth and gravel flying in our faces . . .'

The troops endured sandstorms, nightmarches, intolerable thirst, constant hunger and fatigue, and always there were precipitous crags and rocks to climb and descend and all the time there were the very real dangers of ambush. Casualties were heavy and Colonel Somerset of the 74th was himself killed storming the Amatolas at the head of his men. A vivid record of the campaign was kept, amongst others, by the artist Thomas Baines, who accompanied the 74th, and left many sketches and paintings of this forgotten war.

Castor remained at the Cape for a year, during the period

of the war, and her log makes interesting reading. There are domestic details such as 'issued slop clothing to ship's company, survey on a bale of blue cloth, opened rum 26 = 35 gals., received fresh beef 165 and vegetables 82 lbs., received from Simons Bay victualling office chocolate 313 = 106 lbs., potatoes 112 lbs., preserved meats 155 lbs., issued to Dr. Charles 1 lb., of sugar for the sick, opened pepper 28 lbs,' together with more warlike entries: 'read the articles of war to the ship's company, exercised newly raised men at the broad sword, party employed landing the guns and shot of *Rhadamanthus*, exercised young gentlemen at musket and broad sword.' The young gentlemen appear quite frequently at this exercise—and later at the 'great guns' and also cutlasses. There are other side lights on naval life: 'employed coaling ship, up and moored boats' (a frequent entry), 'fired a royal salute in commemoration of the coronation of Her Most Gracious Majesty Queen Victoria, punished Henry Bowen, boy, with 24 lashes for easing himself on the lower deck and Wm. Strong, boy with 24 lashes for being drunk and vomiting in church when on shore duty.'

By the end of the year, the war was under control, and on 22 December the entry reads 'victualled 3 lieutenants, 1 midshipman, 71 seamen and marines, total 75, from the frontier.' This was the return of the naval brigade.

There is a sad entry on 27 February 1852, 'received the melancholy intelligence of the loss of H.M. Steam troopship *Birkenhead* on Danger Point.'* *Castor* sent a party of rescue

---

*The *Birkenhead*, a steam troopship, was wrecked off Simon's Bay on 26 February 1952. She was carrying drafts of the 12th Lancers, 60th Rifles, 2nd, 6th, 43rd, 45th, 73rd, 74th and 91st Regiments as well as women and children for whom the boats, which could only hold 138 people, were used, saving all of them. Out of 638 people on board 454 were drowned including almost all the troops who had stood fast after the Captain had given the order 'every man for himself,' waiting to be dismissed by their officers. Captain Wright of the 91st and Lieutenant Giradot of the 43rd ordered them to remain where they were as the boats, already very full, would capsize if the men tried to join them. They stood fast until the ship sank under them. Sir Henry Yule commemorated the incident in verse and the King of Prussia ordered an account of it to be read to all regiments in his army.

survivors, and helped to save twenty-five seamen, sixty-three soldiers, seven women and thirteen children.

At last, on 2 April, came the entry 'employed preparing for sea' and on 5 April '6.30 made all plain sail: 7.30 slipped the moorings.'

Between April and September 1852, *Castor* was at sea for much of the time, and the map in the frontispiece of her log shows her cruise up the east coast of Southern Africa to Pemba Bay, eastwards to the Comoro Islands, thence to Mauritius, round the southern tip of Madagascar and back to the Cape. The log shows entries such as 'killed bullocks, pike and carbine drill, marines landed at exercises, boys sent on shore to church' (none got drunk this time—they had learnt their lesson), and then back in Capetown, 'painting ship, party working at the Commodore's house . . .'

Sulivan was now to have two years in home waters before campaigning again, but there was another adventurous experience on the way home in May 1852 on *Megaera*—to which he had transferred at the Cape. Four days after leaving Cape St Vincent, as the ship was doing a good seven knots, the Captain-of-the-Foretop fell into the water, and Sulivan, fully dressed, jumped twenty feet from the poop into the sea, where he seized the man, kept him afloat, and swam to a hastily thrown lifebuoy, where they hung until a ship's boat had been lowered and they were picked up. For this deed he was awarded the silver medal of the Royal Humane Society.

In January 1853, he was appointed Mate, and joined the Royal Steam Yacht *Victoria and Albert*; only nine months later he was promoted Lieutenant, and in the following year, 1854, was once again on active service.

CHAPTER 3

BROTHERS AT WAR, 1854

The Crimean War, the extraordinary war in which Britain overcame her suspicions of Napoleon III's imperial designs and allied herself against Russia with France and Turkey, a country which Tsar Nicholas referred to as 'the Sick Man of Europe,' had more complex causes than those popularly considered at the time. The Russian people may have thought that the war was fought to protect the Orthodox Christian subjects of the Sultan of Turkey against the Roman Catholics supported by France in their dispute over who should place a silver star in the Church of Nativity in Bethlehem or possess a golden key to the door, a quarrel which had led to the killing of two Orthodox monks and the intervention of Muslim police. Some French Catholics may possibly have thought of a modern crusade, but more were reminded of Napoleonic victories half a century before and of an unfulfilled score outstanding against Russia; and some Britons may have thought of justice for the downtrodden Turk. But there is little doubt about what the Admiralty thought. The Tsar was building a great naval base at Sebastopol, from which Constantinople was menaced, and if Constantinople were to fall, the Mediterranean would be dominated by Russia; and if the Mediterranean were thus dominated, the British and their supply lines to the East would be threatened. Once the war was declared, there were two naval objectives: in the Baltic, to curtail the activities of the Russian fleet, and to keep it as far as possible locked up and unable to send reinforcements to the south; and in the south, Sebastopol had to be taken and the naval base captured and destroyed.

Soon after the outbreak of war in 1854, Bartholomew Sulivan sailed from Lowestoft in command of survey ship

Lightning, a three-gun paddle steamer and the first steam vessel to be built for the Navy.

The fleet's orders were to take up a good position in the Baltic, to prevent any Russian ship from escaping into the North Sea, and after the ice had cleared away, to shut up the Russian fleet in the Gulf of Finland. Sulivan's orders, issued by the hydrographer, Sir Francis Beaufort, were to 'assist with the important operations of the Baltic Fleet, by making such skilful and rapid reconnaissances as well as by occasional hydrographic surveys wherever it may be considered necessary.' Finally he was instructed to render everything he did 'more or less subservient to the great object of improving our charts.'

On 2 April, he wrote from Kioze Bay to say that he had just seen a signal from a steamer 'have minister on board with declaration of war.' 'So all hope of peace is over,' he wrote, 'it was sad to think today that the line of beautiful ships surrounded by boats with pleasure parties of the Danes and with steam boats from Copenhagen full of spectators might soon be acting such a different part.'

Old Admiral Napier utilized *Lightning* as a fleet tender, and Sulivan chafed at finding himself in the position of an errand boy, although he continued, as far as possible, to obey the hydrographer's instructions, constantly sounding and checking charts. As always, in all his ships, he held regular services and had an attentive congregation. He was not permitted by the Admiral to reconnoitre Sweaborg,* for he had an enemy at court in the shape of an officer known as the Master of the Fleet, who encouraged the elderly Admiral in his cautiousness. He made reconnaissances of Hango and, whilst trying to get a closer look at the forts in one of the ship's boats, he saw a party of Russian soldiers riding to the point of an island, in order to cut him off—reminiscent of his encounters with cavalry in South America.

There ensued a period of small boat work amongst the innumerable islands, to whose terrified inhabitants he distributed tracts and presented a large Swedish Bible. His

*Now Suomenlinne. It was an island fortress guarding the entrance to Helsingfors (Helsinki).

subsequent report enabled the fleet to move to Bomarsund Bay, but he continued to reconnoitre the many channels between the islands, making sketches and observing enemy soldiers through field glasses, whilst all the time taking a keen interest in the inhabitants, with some of whom he became on friendly terms. In one farmhouse he discovered a remarkable print of Queen Victoria and Prince Albert preparing for a bathe, as well as portraits of the King of Prussia and the Prince and Princess of Sweden. 'The more I see of them,' he wrote, 'the more I am interested in the people. I hope to induce the Admiral to order that no more of their vessels shall be burnt or their property injured.'

Sulivan was given the task of reconnoitring Cronstadt with four ships, three English and one French, with *Lightning* leading. They ran into range of the Russian fleet, consisting of seventeen or eighteen ships, both sail and steam, and withdrew fairly rapidly, having seen all that was necessary. This was followed by a period of intense reconnoitring activity, for at last the Admiral had seen the value of having a competent surveyor in these most difficult waters.

Sulivan next sailed to Sweaborg under a flag of truce, to talk to the Russians about exchanges of prisoners, and—true to character—refused to have angles taken, drawings made, or even allow a leadsman in the chains, as he was under a flag of truce and thought this would be dishonourable.

His next task was to lead the fleet into Bomarsund through Led Sound 'through channels so narrow that the line of battle ships seemed like giants looking down on the small islands.' He went to the village of Degerby where he made friends, but arrested the local police officer who had been forbidding the villagers to sell produce to the allies. Amongst these friends were some of the local ladies of whom he had a party of six to lunch, and whose acquaintance he renewed with several subsequent visits. Most of the time, though, he was kept hard at work piloting ships of the fleet; the French Admiral said he thought Sulivan 'must be made of iron.' Meanwhile, there was a build-up of French soldiers on the British ships and 'it was a curious sight,' he wrote (thirty-nine years after Waterloo) 'seeing a thousand French soldiers

paraded on the deck of an English ninety-gun ship. They
have got on capitally, all pleasant and mutually pleased.' The
Russian forts were still untouched and whenever Sulivan was
piloting vessels anywhere near the range of the guns they
would open up and try to reach them 'both by riccochet and
direct line.'

On 2 August, he had a most impressive reconnoitring
party on board *Lightning*: Napier and Duchesne, the French
Commanding General, four other French Generals, General
Jones, and innumerable Colonels and Staff Officers. 'They
crowded our deck under the awning from the mainmast to
the wheel.' He took *Lightning* in to what he thought was a
hundred yards out of range of the forts, but as the great ones
all studied it through glasses and drew plans, Russian shot
screamed overhead. Had it found its target that would indeed have been a bullseye—and all Sulivan's fault for under-
estimating the range of one of the big guns. They were fired
on again navigating the channel out, but the shot dropped
harmlessly short. The French were most impressed at
Sulivan's knowledge of the intricate channels and the
existence of rocks, and one of them compared him to a dog
nosing out truffles. After several hectic days of introducing
other captains and masters to the navigational hazards, he
found himself—in *Lightning*—leading a small fleet of
steamers, including three French ones, amongst them old
Fulton of Parana days, through the channels, laden with
eighteen hundred French troops and eight hundred British
marines and sappers to a landing point selected by Sulivan
north of Bomarsund. At the same time another French force
landed further south.

It was a strange sort of war that Sulivan described:

all the troops advanced without firing a shot, and closed
the enemy up in their forts . . . we were landing guns,
stores, etc., the forts sending only an occasional shot or
shell inland. The marines and seamen were rather exposed
about fifteen hundred yards from the fort on the hill. The
marines had bought a potato field for £3 from the owners
and were digging potatoes when a shell burst in the valley,

scattering balls six ounces in weight . . . I walked out to see the camp that evening . . . the French advanced chasseurs hidden under rocks on a rise of ground; the pack artillery behind some rocks ready for placing in battery . . . the round fort on the hill looking down on all within good range but only firing an occasional shot or shell. At the village Headquarters there was a beautiful band playing while the general was at dinner . . . several native women mixed with the soldiers, listening . . . which I was glad to see as it showed they were not ill-treated. People were at work getting in their hay and corn in one field . . .

After the French shore bombardment and the chasseurs' accurate rifle shots at the casements, the west fort surrendered. Sulivan took leave from the Admiral to go ashore to see the action and the effect of ships' gunfire at long range on the fort. He had a very close escape when the west tower exploded . . . 'It was an awful moment . . . masses of stones were flying beyond our position.' However, by watching the stones descend and dodging the big ones he managed to escape injury, and attached himself to a French chasseur who had a safe nook between two rocks, from whence he fired at the casements. He then went on to look at the English breaching battery, composed mainly of sailors. But Sulivan was no fire eater, and 'thought much of the hours of the following day if the forts were to be stormed and prayed that the Almighty would guide those on whom it depended to prevent the necessity of it taking place.' Fortunately his prayers were answered and the Russian general surrendered.

Despite his humanitarianism, he had an ingenuous interest in the fruits of glory, and his memoirs are interspersed with the good reports that he hears of himself, the possibility of a French award of the *Légion d'Honneur*, the good will of the Admiral . . . and as in the Parana campaign he allows himself some bitterness at the lack of recognition and regard that he received. Meanwhile, he would countenance no overt criticism of higher authority, and in order to get rid of a journalist—the correspondent of the *Morning Herald*—he gave him his 'opinion on the subject of newspapers and their correspondents and the falsehoods they publish, on the system of puffing some parties that was springing up in a way that will get me anything but favourably mentioned . . . there are parties in the fleet in league with these reporters for the sake of getting themselves puffed.'

There was another reconnaissance, this time to Revel, where they again contacted the Russians under flag of truce, to discuss the wounded Russian prisoners. The Russian party came out on a steam frigate, and Sulivan wrote 'I had no idea they had such a beautiful vessel . . . in beautiful order' and a 'fine, handsome, gentlemanly young lieutenant' brought a letter for Sir Charles Napier.

Meanwhile, off Bomarsund, the French troops were being decimated by cholera and already seven hundred out of ten thousand had been buried. Sulivan thought that the damp ground on which the troops lay, or else their habit of 'eating every green thing they could lay hold of' was the cause, but there was not a single case on board *Lightning*, although she was anchored between Presto Island and the fort, less than a hundred yards from each shore, where the French were dying on each side.

In England there was some public demand that the fleet should take Cronstadt, and Sulivan was at pains to point out that 'these opinions are from people sitting down at a desk,' and that Cronstadt was a very difficult nut, with forts on all sides. 'What the newspapers say in leading articles . . . is great nonsense and only misleads people. If our fleet had madly tried to attack Cronstadt and had been beaten and partly destroyed, as it must have been, the papers would have been the first to cry out about knocking our ships to pieces against stone walls.' However, there were still Revel and Sweaborg, and once again Sulivan took a party of Admirals and a General to reconnoitre Revel, 'a very strong place . . . folly to attack it with ships. I wish,' he wrote 'some of those fighting newspapermen were put into a ship by themselves, and anchored off one of these batteries to have their full of it; they would then know a little more on the subject (those that were left) than they do now and would not write such utter folly and nonsense.'

Off Sweaborg, there was a very nasty moment when a party including Sir Charles Napier nearly came to grief. Sulivan had been in and out of the anchorage several times and was reasonably confident, although he knew by the Russian charts there was a rock outside the anchorage of whose exact position he was unaware. 'It was very different turning a steamer of a-thousand-and-fifty tons (they were in *Driver*) and I took every care. Scarcely moving now and then to keep her way; but the engine stopped as we turned, when, instead of being outside this rock, as I thought, we were between it and the island . . . we were in such a position that I dare not go astern for fear of going on other rocks, and there was no chance for turning her on a pivot in the spot she was . . . it was an anxious few minutes everybody watching eagerly but not saying a word . . . they (i.e. Russians) would certainly take us before ships could get from Nargen to help us. Having four big officers under my charge did not of course lessen the anxiety. However in a few minutes (during which you might have heard a pin drop almost when the engines were stopped) she turned right round and came out as we went in all right. The old Chief (Admiral Napier), generally so nervous, behaved very well . . . and said 'Upon my word, you did it uncommonly well: if you had not, I should dine in Helsingfors today.'

Shortly after this incident, Sulivan went walking across the island at the entrance to Sweaborg, where he met an old woman who had washed for Nelson's officers in 1802.

On leave in England, he drew up a report, at the request of the First Lord, on the feasibility of attacking Cronstadt and Sweaborg, by a combined naval and military force, or by a naval force alone, as well as the practicability of confining attentions solely to a blockade. He drew up a plan to bombard Sweaborg following on an attack on Cronstadt further north, using the floating batteries that were then being built. The Admiralty sanctioned this scheme, which also included a quite remarkable plan in which he and his brother, George, were to play the leading roles. In order to carry out the necessary survey of the channel almost up to the walls of Cronstadt, the two brothers were to set forth in a double canoe, from which they were to swim the last part, clad in oilskin swimsuits lined with wool to resist the cold, with pockets for holding small sounding lines and lead. In the end the attack on Cronstadt was abandoned for the time being and the floating batteries were sent to the Black Sea to join the fleet in which George was serving.

Here at Odessa, the fleet under Admiral Dundas, comprising twenty ships of the line and twelve steam frigates, including George's ship *Vesuvius*, cleared for action and the Russian Governor was ordered to send away all neutral ships and to surrender all Russian ships. As Count Osten-Sackedey only released the neutral ships, the terms were deemed not to have been complied with, and the bombardment was opened by *Samaon*, a six-gun paddle steamer similar to *Vesuvius*. She and the sixteen-gun *Tiger* operated inshore, immune from enemy fire; the fifty-gun 4th rate *Arethusa*, stood in from shore under full sail, holding her fire until within short range, despite fire from Russian batteries, and then destroyed a Russian mortar battery on the heights above the town, by firing broadside from the port guns, tacking, firing with the bow guns as she came about, then a broadside with starboard guns before tacking again and opening up with the stern guns, repeating three times this classic manoeuvre of the days of sail, the last occasion in history when a sailing frigate bombarded a shore target. Later, the small rocket boats went in close and fired at Russian ships in the harbour, firing a number of them and starting conflagrations in the town. Counter fire was returned by Russian horse artillery who galloped up and unlimbered on the mole. At noon the fleet withdrew out of range, whilst the fires in the town spread rapidly. After an afternoon's bombardment, the British ships opened up again and withdrew in the evening.

The first specific mention of *Vesuvius* in the 'Correspondence between the Admiralty and Vice-Admiral Dundas relative to Naval Operations in the Black Sea' comes in June 1854. An allied army had been sent to the Gallipoli Peninsula, where the notorious Scutari Barracks hospital was later to be made famous by Florence Nightingale. The fleet of transports sailed from thence to Varna on the Black

Sea coast of Bulgaria in order to protect the port in case the Turks, who were also fighting the Russians in Silistria, were forced back to the line of the Danube. In the event, the Russians retreated and *Vesuvius*, together with *Firebrand* and *Fury*, was sent to cruise off the mouth of the Danube in order to watch the coast and send reports of enemy troop movements. Although the Russians continued to withdraw, the bulk of the French army was moved to Varna, bringing with it the cholera that had broken out en route from Marseilles. This spread to the British troops and to the fleet, whose base was at Balchik Bay, fifteen miles up the coast of the north. The fleets put to sea but carried the disease with them. *Britannia*, the flag ship, had one hundred and nine deaths in two days, and ships were worked by severely reduced crews. Meanwhile the British and French armies played only a minimal part in harassing the Russians and by August there was no further reason for remaining in the unhealthy districts around Varna.

On 24 June, the allied armies began to embark in Balchik Bay; their destination, the Crimea. The strategic objective of this move was to capture the Russian naval base and fortress of Sebastopol and to destroy the Russian Black Sea Fleet. It took ten days to embark twenty-four thousand infantry, one thousand cavalry and their horses, and sixty guns and their limbers with six hundred horses. The convoy sailed on 6 September, five columns of merchantmen with thirty ships in each column, with unattached steamers and escort ships surrounding them. Sailing at the speed of the slowest sailing vessels, they took four days and nights to cover the three-hundred miles to the rendezvous with the French and Turkish ships west of Cape Tarka, the westernmost promontory of the Crimean Peninsula, and on the 12th, the allied armada sailed into Calamita Bay, seventy miles south of the town of Eupatoria, and began disembarking troops the next day. On to the beaches of the Crimea were disgorged sixty thousand men, British, French and Turks, ablaze in every colour of the rainbow, in reds, blues, golds, as on parade grounds; in shakos, breast plates and bearskins: this was the last great military kaleidoscope the world was to see, and these men in their magnificent uniforms were themselves to become, before the year was out, weary, bearded veterans, their tattered greatcoats insufficient to protect them from the intense cold of the Crimean winter.

On 16 September, *Vesuvius* was sent by the Commander-in-Chief, in company with *Retribution*, to Eupatoria, where they found the town to be defenceless. The crews landed in order 'to concert means for the defence of the town and bay from incursions or attacks from the enemy; the inhabitants have received them very well and a police has been established,' wrote Admiral Dundas to the Secretary to the Admiralty on 18 September, the day before the allied armies started to move off towards Sebastopol, on a beautiful September morning, with the bands playing, the French on the right, divisions dispersed in diamond formation, and the British square on the left. Meanwhile, the fleets kept the Russians in Sebastopol under surveillance and sent word to the armies when they saw a Russian army move north to meet the allies at the river Alma, half-way between the landing beaches and their objective of Sebastopol.

At midday on 20 September, the sixty thousand men of the allied armies halted on the Crimean steppe and for the first time surveyed their enemy, drawn up on the heights two miles further north. Between the armies lay the river and here in the Valley of the Alma was fought the first battle of the war. Only a mile or two upstream from the mouth of the river, off which *Vesuvius* was cruising, the French General Canrobert took his division across the fords, to turn the Russian flank. In the centre was Prince Jerome Napoleon with the British army on the left. Lord Raglan, the Commander-in-Chief and the French General St Armand were each with their staffs in the centre of the armies. Lord Raglan and his staff of mounted officers in cocked hats and plumes rode up and down the lines, attracting Russian attention, and as the British came under fire from the great and lesser redoubts, they waited patiently for the order to attack once the French had gained the top of the cliffs and had engaged the Russian flank. At last the order came, and the great lines of scarlet-coated men steadily advanced, although the cannon balls and musketry felled many of them. The men of the Light division captured the great redoubt, later to be stormed again by the Russians before the British main army retook it and the Russians withdrew towards Sebastopol. The British had four hundred men killed and over one thousand five hundred men wounded, whilst the French losses were sixty killed and more than four hundred wounded.

The Russians took with them an unknown number of wounded but some they had to leave behind, and the next reference to *Vesuvius* in Admiral Dundas's despatches is in connection with these. Addressed from *Britannia*, off the Katscha, and dated 28 September 1854, it reads:

> *Albion* and *Vesuvius* returned last night from off the Alma river, having brought down from the country and embarked on board *Avon* transport, about three-hundred-and-forty wounded Russians, whom I immediately sent on in charge of Commander Rogers of the *Albion* with a letter to the Governor of Odessa. From the state of the country, Captain Lushington was obliged to use every precaution in protecting his people employed on this service, and yesterday afternoon he was forced to embark all his men under the guns of *Vesuvius* as a body of about 6,000 Russians had advanced rapidly upon them.

Dundas ends his despatch by writing 'the cholera is showing itself occasionally among the ships of the fleet, but the crews generally are healthy . . .,' and the sixty-nine year old British Admiral showed humanity in the letter that he wrote to General Annenhof, Governor of Odessa:

> I have the honour to inform your Excellency that in consequence of the advance on Sebastopol of the Allied Armies after the battle of the Alma of the 20th instant, a number of wounded Russian officers and soldiers were left in the rear in the small villages near the places where they had fallen: and by the request of His Excellency General Lord Raglan I have collected as many as I could (about 340). In order to shorten the sufferings of these gallant soldiers which a long sea voyage must necessarily

increase, I have sent them to Odessa rather than to Constantinople, the distance to the former being so much less.

He did not add that they might not have fared so well in the care of our Turkish allies.

Meanwhile, the Russian army withdrew southwards in some disorder, Prince Menshikov and even General Gortchakoff tramping alone and on foot towards Sebastopol, where Admiral Korniloff had sunk a line of ships across the harbour mouth. The allies advanced to the Belbek river, the last of the four rivers that had separated them from their beaches in the north and Sebastopol to the south. It was to take them a year to cover those four miles; a year in which they encircled and invested the garrison from the south, convinced that a direct attack from the north would fail, although Prince Menshikov was convinced that he could not, in fact, defend Sebastopol from the north. The sailors from the Russian ships sunk across the harbour were used to take over the town's defences, as Menshikov's plan was for the army to move northwards to keep the supply routes open. The two armies passed within a short distance of each other, the British heading south for Balaclava, a little harbour on the coast, so that Sebastopol was encircled, although the main Russian army lay outside the circle. The French joined forces with the British whilst surveying vessels sounded the entrance to the harbour.

In Sebastopol, the Russians were fortunate in their commanders: Admirals Kornilov and Nachinov, General Moller who had 3,000 men detached by mistake from the main Russian army, and the great engineer Todleben. The defences were strengthened with ingenuity and vigour. The guns were stripped from the ships and the whole garrison worked at it. The allies slowly—far too slowly—made their preparations, and on 17 October the British and the French between them had moved one hundred and twenty-six guns in an arc around the town, their main targets the flagstaff Bastion and the Redan and on that day the great land bombardment opened up at half-past-six in the morning—the heaviest ever known. One thousand one hundred

Russians were killed, but Sebastopol remained in enemy hands.

Meanwhile, at sea, *Vesuvius* had been kept busy in the two weeks preceding the bombardment. On the 3rd, together with *Tribune* and a French squadron, she had accompanied Admiral Dundas from Balaclava to Yalta, on the south-east coast of the Crimean Peninsula where the boats of the united squadron landed marines and sailors who took the town, whilst a small number of cossacks and infantry marched out. Admiral Dundas wrote—

Our expedition (i.e. for foraging) has, I fear, been a failure. The French have shipped about 400 sacks of such bad flour that the Commissary would have nothing to do with it, about thirty bullocks and seventeen small barrels of wine . . . The flour . . . is what they make the soldiers' black bread from. I assisted in shipping it but after hoisting some 60 bags into the *Golden Fleece*, I sent specimens of it to the French Admiral who agreed with me that our forces could make no use of it. The bullocks and wine were found only after long search round the country houses which had better be avoided unless we were sure of more successful results, for they lead to drunkenness and pillage in spite of every precaution. We are here in a bad neighbourhood for temptation—on one side a beautiful villa of the Empress, and on the other a shooting lodge of Prince Voronzov, which was last visited this morning, but Captain Carnegie having wisely put English sentries on the doors, only some storehouses suffered in loss of sugar, etc. Commander Powell (*Vesuvius*'s Captain) and myself found a small store of coals which was intended for the use of the Russian steamers; this, which amounts to 35 tons, I have shipped on board the *Vesuvius* and have told the Commander to paste against this door '35 tons of coal (Imperial property) taken by English men of war.' I have purchased a large quantity of plank which I think may be wanted for platforms. I have therefore put it on *Vesuvius* and have directed that vessel to proceed with it to Balaclava . . . I have just returned from the shore, and having met the Steward of Prince Voronzov who takes

oath that the coals are his master's property, I directed
Commander Powell to give him receipts for the quantity
embarked.

Dundas was a gentleman of the old school who respected the
rights of other gentlemen.

Vesuvius returned to Balaclava where she offloaded her
strange cargo and then steamed to Sebastopol roads, where
the fleets of four countries were converging. The British
Black Sea Fleet had eleven ships of the line, of which
Agamemnon, one of the first of the new ninety-one-gun
steam first rates, was the flag ship of Rear-Admiral Sir
Edmund Lyons, Commander of the inshore squadron.
Britannia, one hundred and twenty-guns, was Dundas' flag
ship. There were forty frigates altogether, in both the main
division and the inshore squadron, of which thirty were
steam vessels, including *Vesuvius*. The French had fifteen
ships of the line and twenty-one frigates, of which thirteen
were steam-powered, and the Russians also had fifteen ships
of the line, seven frigates and seventeen corvettes. Five of the
line of battle ships and two of the frigates had been sunk as
block ships on 24 September. There was also a Turkish
squadron under a Rear-Admiral, which played a minor role
in the bombardment.

On the night of 16 October, a daring survey, similar to
some of those undertaken by Bartholomew Sulivan in the
Baltic, was carried out by three ships' masters, who, under
cover of darkness, had discovered a channel through the
dangerous shoal which ran right out to sea in front of Fort
Constantine. Slowly, with muffled oars, they were rowed
within the line of enemy look-out boats, and charted the
channel through which the next day the bombarding vessels
were slowly tugged. The four steam frigates, *Sphinx*,
Terrible, *Tribune* and *Sampson* gave covering fire as
Agamemnon went first, followed by *Sanspareil*, then
London (destined to become the most famous of all vessels
connected with the East African slavery trade and to be
commanded by Sulivan twenty years later), *Britannia*, and
Queen towed by *Vesuvius*, followed by *Trafalgar*,
Vengeance, *Bellerophon* and *Rodney*, forming by two

o'clock (a long time after the military bombardment) a great arc of warships stretching for two miles across the road-steads. The British on the left came under fire from the two great forts of Nicholas and Paul, built on promontories at the entrance of the inner harbour, as well as from the Russian fleet. *Sanspareil*, *Agamemnon*, *London* were all hit; *Bellerophon* was set on fire and so was *Queen* when she sailed up to assist, and *Rodney* went aground. Two Russian batteries known as the Wasp and the Telegraph were the ones that did the damage, perched on the edge of the cliffs above Fort Constantine. They had an officer, in full view of the British Fleet, who stood there with his quadrant, plotting the distance for the shells which were fired with time fuses. The Turkish and French ships were anchored well out in deep water and apart from a hit on *Ville de Paris*, the flag ship of Vice-Admiral Hamelin, they suffered little damage, but the British were less fortunate. Whilst the ships of the line were being towed by the steamers, in the absence of wind, several were hit and set on fire. Then with the steam vessels lashed to their port beam, the starboard guns of the ships of the line engaged the enemy. This was George Sulivan's first taste of real warfare, for the enemy returned accurate fire. The Fleet continued to pound away, and to be pounded, until 6.30 pm. Their fire power was considerably reduced by the absence of many of the guns, serving with the land bombardment, and the upper decks of many were denuded.

The land and sea bombardment which had occupied most of the day was not followed up by an assault, although Raglan had proposed this to the French Marshall Canrobert after the tower of the Malakov had been knocked down and a breach made in the Redan.

Admiral Dundas wrote to the Admiralty the next day: 'An action of this duration against such formidable and well-armed works could not be maintained without serious injury, and I have to regret the loss of forty-four killed and two-hundred-and-sixty-six wounded . . . The ships, masts, yards and rigging are more or less damaged, principally by shells and hot shot.'

Less than a week after this, the Russians attempted to cut

off Balaclava from the rest of the British forces, and this was to result, on 25 October, in the famous charges of the Heavy Brigade, which drew the enemy back, and Cardigan's charge of the Light Brigade, which achieved little and left the Russians in control of the Voronzov road running east to west, north of the harbour, thus ensuring great privation for the British army during the coming winter. This was followed on 5 November by the battle of Inkerman, where the Russians were defeated on the heights to the east of Sebastopol.

Not long after this, in mid-November, the allied fleet suffered serious damage to ships, and considerable loss of life, in a disastrous hurricane that struck Eupatoria; five transports were blown on to the shore and many more warships suffered damage, including *Vesuvius*, which was dismasted.

Between November and May, whilst the terrible Crimean winter was taking its toll of allied soldiers, when Russell of *The Times* was sending home his despatches to bring for the first time the real details of war into the homes of the civilian population, and when Florence Nightingale was creating some order out of chaos, the navy continued to play its role of watching the coast line, protecting transports, landing small bodies of troops, blockading and continuing the innumerable maritime chores of a supporting role. In November 1854, in a despatch from Captain Simmons to Lord Raglan, it is mentioned that all the works on the Sulina had been destroyed and George Sulivan was mentioned in despatches for his share in the action.

Meanwhile, a continent away to the north, Bartholomew had returned to the Baltic, this time in command of *Merlin*, larger than *Lightning*, a paddle steamer with six guns, and as the attack to be mounted on Sweaborg was largely his plan, he wrote 'my chief anxiety is lest I may not have the power to carry it all out as I wish or lest I may not have the means to ensure success and yet get the blame for any failure.' He also wrote

Oh, how thankful should I be to have all my plans frustrated at the eleventh hour by peace! I know it is, apparently, impossible now; but I recollect how impossible it seemed that the scene of slaughter arranged for the next day at Bomarsund could be avoided and yet in half an hour it was prevented by the surrender. If war is still to go on, then we must endeavour to feel that God has some wise purpose in permitting it and that all is for the best.

Once again he took the Admirals and their staffs to look at Revel, where there were new fortifications, and at Sweaborg where they were watched by 'thousands of both sexes . . . every hill and rise were crowded with people.'

He went ashore to his old stamping grounds at Nargen and met the women to whom he had given a Bible and was interested to note that the children, even a six-year old, could read. On the village green a cricket match took place between the officers of *Cressy* and *Royal George*.

Nearly all in red, pink, or blue flannel shirts, which have generally superseded white ones in the fleet . . . All looked so cheerful and pretty, with the fine buildings and towers of Revel in front of us that I could not help thinking 'can this be wartime?' The weather and the whole scene were much too lovely to be broken in on by the horrors of war. What a mercy it will be if yet at the eleventh hour we have peace.

Here again, he distributed Bibles.

At Viborg Bay, *Merlin* with *Magicienne* under command captured seven small vessels, whose crews were made prisoner and who were later killed by Russian troops when a landing party took them to Hango, under a flag of truce, which the Russian officer in charge of the soldiers ashore refused to respect. Sulivan thought that the Finnish militia were responsible and that this was because of the ill-feeling the Finns had for the English after 'the destruction of their private property last year by Admiral Plumridge in so wanton a manner . . . so terribly do unjust acts lead to retribution.'

Once again off Cronstadt he noted that on the island two miles from the town, 'a series of large earthen batteries have

been built, extending right across the island, adding greatly
to the strength of the place, as no ships can get near them,'
and no army could get within range of Cronstadt till these
works were taken. It was a beautiful evening and the sun lit
up 'the gilded steeples of Cronstadt, St Petersburg (very
distant, but just seen), and the palace at Perhoff most
beautifully . . .'

The next day, again with the Admirals on board, they went
round the north side of the island, where they saw four sail
of the line, six frigates and two corvettes moored as block
ships inside the barrier and twenty four gun boats which did
nothing to stop the intruders. The following day he and two
Admirals even pulled for the shore in the gig and whale boat.
A week later he had his first experience of an 'infernal
machine' as the early mines were called. There were two
explosions, the second of which occurred just in front of the
starboard paddle upon which the artist from the *Illustrated
London News* was sitting making his sketches—fortunately
with no damage to himself or his drawings. Below decks the
engineers' mess was wrecked. However, this was not to prove
so serious as a subsequent encounter that *Vulture* had some
days later. Sulivan had led the fleet up to a position off the
north side of Cronstadt island when *Vulture*, in the middle of
the fleet, exploded an 'infernal.' Everyone started searching
in ship's boats for more of these things and Admiral
Seymour himself helped to haul one into his gig. He took it
to the poop of his ship where it exploded, injuring him
seriously and wounding several others. Altogether, twenty-
four 'infernals' were fished out.

Yet another reconnaissance of Cronstadt revealed that the
Russians had seven two-deckers, seven large frigates and five
corvettes as block ships moored in line; behind them were
twenty three screw gun boats, a great many row gun boats
and thirteen small steamers; and further inland were a screw
frigate, four paddle frigates and two or three sloop steamers.
'To force this and make a gap we have at most fifteen gun
boats and one or two small steamers; all the others drew too
much water . . . even if the floating batteries cross they
would never stand such a tremendous force . . . yet there are

wiseacres who abuse us for not taking Cronstadt . . .'

The projected assault on Cronstadt was abandoned, and the counsels of war next considered Sweaborg. 'The French chief has wished to bombard Helsingfors, the town at Sweaborg and not the fortress. This, I think, would be almost a cruelty to destroy private houses, churches, observatory etc., particularly with a large fortress full of docks, buildings, barracks etc., close at hand—a legitimate object of attack.'

On one occasion he reached the sound inside Wormso island, and by looking over the bows of one of the two gun boats with *Merlin* (for whom it was too shallow, being only eight feet deep), Sulivan steered between the stones and got both boats, drawing seven feet each, up the channel to the town of Hapsal, 'the Brighton of Russia,' as he termed it! 'There were large crowds of people, large parties of ladies with parasols of all colours.'

'On proceeding towards Dago, after lying quiet all Sunday' (as Sulivan invariably did when circumstances permitted, when he could have 'his boys,' as he called them, in to a Bible reading session), he followed a small cutter into a cove and set fire to her. Not long afterwards he met her owner Baron Sternberg, and this led to some amiable and civilised encounters between enemies. The Baron, a personable young man of thirty-five, the proprietor of the island of Dago, had refused to organize the five thousand able-bodied men into a militia at the request of the Russian general, knowing this would provoke attack. Sulivan was driven in the Baron's carriage to his castle, sitting beside the Baroness, a young lady of about twenty-two. It was a 'splendid house, shaded over the entrance by fine horse-chestnuts, beautiful grounds round, and inside like a handsome English country house.' The drawing-room was so beautiful that Sulivan thought himself in fairyland, but he thought the flowers in the garden compared unfavourably with similar ones in England. The stables were good, full of fine horses, stout island ponies, and the Baroness's thoroughbred English mare. The Baron also had an English riding horse as well as carriage horses.

It all seemed like a dream: three miles inland in an enemy's country and going over all these quite English-like scenes with a nice young lady speaking as good English as I did, having been entirely educated by an English governess. She expressed surprise that the English had not burnt Hapsal which had been full of the principal families from St Petersburg, including the wife and daughters of the General commanding, who, fearing that Revel would be bombarded, had assumed that Hapsal was too shallow for the British fleet.

Sulivan tried to explain that despite incidents which he deplored, the British had no wish to harm civilians. After a splendid dinner, rounded off with coffee and tea under a tree, the guests were driven back to their ship by the Baron who told Sulivan that the salt trade in the small boats carried on by the poor fishermen of the islands was their livelihood, and that many of the inhabitants were dependent on salt fish and pledged his word that none would be sent to the mainland if the Admiral lifted the blockade, but Sulivan could promise nothing.

The next day the Baron lunched aboard and once again took a naval party off to dinner. The Baroness had just heard from her sister at Hapsal, who said that their grand ball had been held on the evening that Sulivan had led the ships up close, and many ladies had packed up and gone before this ball, to which Sulivan replied that he was sorry he had not been given an invitation!

Back at the fleet, he found himself much sought after by fellow Captains who thought he would have a deciding voice in the disposition for the bombardment of Sweaborg, and who hoped to take part; he himself hoped that it would never take place, despite his recent award of the C.B.:

when I think of the prolonged horrors at Sebastopol and the destruction and loss that may be caused here, even in a city, I cannot but wish that our government had agreed to Lord John's views (Lord John Russell), and accepted the terms proposed . . . To see us today with our church flags up, and the enemy's also, both professing to serve the same Master—a Master of peace; and to see them toiling all day raising works to defend these buildings, and we striving to reduce them to a heap of ruins! It is very sad; and though never had, as a nation, greater cause for war, a fearful responsibility will rest on any who accomplish the objects for which we entered into it. Had we never sent that expedition to Sebastopol we should have had peace now; and had we confined ourselves to removing the enemy from Turkish ground and then merely blockading closely, we should have saved nearly all the blood and sickness and half the expense, while there would have been no point of honour or heroic defence to raise the national spirit of the Russian people. I cannot but feel we are all now going on with the war because we do not know how to give it up.

He now concentrated on the plan for the bombardment of Sweaborg, and after three days and nights surveying places for the fleet clear of rocks, and charting positions, he piloted the British and French fleets in. Although in essence his plan of attack had been adopted, he was not given the command, and this led to great difficulties as his plan was neither fully understood, nor, in the event, fully carried out. His intention was to anchor mortar vessels six hundred yards outside their eventual positions, to be out of range until just before the action began. Then, after dusk, they were to haul in their kedge anchors, which would bring them in to the precise distance of three thousand three hundred yards, requisite for opening fire. The mortar vessels anchored in a curved line, and four frigates behind them, but the Admiral in charge then ordered them all to be moved further out. Sulivan thereupon put one of his own officers in each frigate, instructing each to weigh anchor, turn the ships head-off a little and drop anchor again without moving the ship her own length, but when he was asked to move the mortar vessels also, he flatly refused. Even so, that night, he found a number of them wrongly moored, because his plan had not been adhered to, and he took it upon himself, without higher orders, to redirect them. Later he wrote 'the experience gained at Sweaborg should be a lesson to any officer who, having proposed a plan of attack, finds it is to be adopted. No delicacy to others, or hesitation in being firm with his superior officers should prevent his insisting that he should be allowed to conduct the proceedings he was responsible for.'

Nevertheless, on 11 August 1855, he was to write

> Thank God with me for a bloodless victory—on our side at least, but I fear not so for the enemy.* Sweaborg is in ruins after two days bombardment and not a scratch on our side . . . it is a special Providence apparently that preserved our people in the little vessels amid showers of shot falling among them and I have to be thankful that I am again spared though in much danger. All has far exceeded my expectations for hardly a building is left except as blackened walls, and such fires are seldom seen. It is almost enough to excite my pride to hear what all are saying about my work . . . I cannot describe to you my feelings—not, I assure you, those of pride, for when all was finished at last, and I went below, the conflicting feelings of gratitude and pleasure were such that, when I went on my knees to offer thanks to the God who still so wonderfully aids me about my deserts, in spite of my neglect of Him, I could only burst into tears.

For days Sulivan had been the moving spirit of the enterprise, reconnoitring, sounding and 'creeping for infernals,' explaining the plan to British and French officers, acting without orders when he saw his plan misunderstood and misinterpreted. Everything had depended on his calculations, for if the mortar vessels had been too close, they would have been destroyed, and if too far, they would not have made the range. However, all was well, and when the action began, after an anxious thirty-seconds of waiting, there was 'a little cloud of smoke, with some fragments of a roof, just in the right position.' Fire was returned from shore batteries, but the British and French gun vessels began to

---

*The Finnish prisoners were taken to England and placed in Lewes jail, but their incarceration was not too onerous and the officers were socially much in demand. Twenty-eight of these prisoners of war are buried in the cemetery of St John sub Castro.

close the range, and to return accurate fire. All the while the crescent of mortar vessels were lobbing shells at the defences and at about ten o'clock, a magazine blew up, followed by another a few hours later, and in a whole series of great explosions, the new earthen battery on top of Gustaf Island vanished, leaving only green turf and rubble, and the buildings on Vago Island were ruins.

That night Sulivan advised the Admiral to move four mortar vessels close in so as to bombard the island of Svento, but this was less successful, again owing to misunderstandings. All night Sulivan was in *Merlin*, or on his gig going from boat to boat. At one time he was annoyed to see that several gun boats had left their proper stations and had crowded amongst the mortar vessels, in such a cluster that the Russians were pounding at them.

> Shots were dropping in all directions, splashing the water against the vessels' sides, and occasionally, though very rarely, one going into a gun boat. In one of the mortar boats I was standing talking to the Captain of the Fleet, my gig close alongside, when one of the large mortar shells plumped down close to us, about three feet from the side and close to my gig's stern.

Firing went on all the next day; the day before they had mostly been 'grand public buildings' that had been destroyed, but this day there were mostly wooden sheds, gun boat sheds, stores for combustibles and arsenals, so that 'the space between the islands was one dense mass of fire by night time.'

On the next day, all was over, and 'we had a nice quiet forenoon, and I think I never saw the crew more impressed with the Service. I did not omit adding thanksgiving for the great mercies we had received.'

There was now talk of a similar bombardment of Helsingfors which Sulivan opposed first on professional grounds . . .

> We should have to go half the distance from the batteries which were at Sweaborg, and then with no good mortars would have to depend principally on our rockets for

burning the town and the only part that we could reach
would be the poorer part of dwelling houses.

His main objection though was that

> on far higher motives I have always opposed it. I think it
> far more honourable for us, a Christian nation, to spare
> the city of private property while we destroy the fortress
> and arsenal . . . If cities and towns are to be destroyed
> when a fleet can reach them, why not every city or town on
> shore that an invading army marches into? I hope we shall
> never set an example of destroying coast towns or war
> will become more barbarous than it was fifty years
> since . . .

After the bombardment of Sweaborg, however, there was
no further major action in the Baltic war. Sulivan, in *Merlin*,
continued to chart and to survey, and to be interested in the
fate of the inhabitants of the many islands: 'I wish the poor
fishermen at Dago and other places could be allowed salt for
their own use to cure fish for this winter, as their sufferings
will be terrible, and this will have no effect on the war either
way . . .' On one occasion he landed at Wormso island and
was taken to the house of Baron Stakleberg, smaller and less
splendidly furnished than Baron Sternberg's, but still
delightful. He was introduced to the family's English
governess, Miss Cooper, who had spent twenty years in
Russia and now spoke with a slightly foreign accent. As with
the Sternbergs, it was the Baroness, rather than the Baron
(who in this case was an Estonian) who was 'the politician of
the party.' 'When I said I hoped the fall of Sebastopol might
lead to peace soon, she quite fired up, struck her little fist on
the table and the fire seemed to flash out of her bright eyes,
as she said, "What! Peace now? *NO, never*, till we have
driven you out of the Crimea again".'

The next day, he and Hewett, his second-in-command,
were taken by the Baron's carriage up to the house for
dinner, and they had a long chat. Miss Cooper took the
Illustrated London News regularly, but whole paragraphs
had been cut by the Censor. Sulivan brought with him the
same numbers of the journal, and all were interested to see

that the forbidden parts were all connected with the late
Tsar, or the Russian objects of the war.

A subsequent dinner party was even more entertaining for
Sulivan took not only the senior officer of one of the French
gun boats ('thinking he would be more likely, if he met the
Baron, to prevent his crews committing any depredations on
the people, which, like some of our own, the Frenchmen are
rather apt to do'), but also the Queen's nephew, Lieutenant
the Prince Ernest of Leiningen, whose mother had been a
near neighbour of the Baron's in Switzerland. Before dining
they had driven to a church on the island, in order to take
observations from the steeple which had

> some doubtful looking fir pegs sticking out to form a
> ladder . . . to get up this with a sextant was no easy
> matter. Up in the top there were merely a few pieces of
> wood across and some loose boards, the diameter of the
> spire there being about five feet. The boards were the
> nesting places of numerous birds, apparently jackdaws,
> and there through a hole I got the observations, the Prince
> also getting up with the spy glass and book writing down
> the angles for me . . .

it was a unique surveying 'cruise,' some miles inland in an
enemy's country driven in a carriage-and-six, accompanied
by a Russian baron, a Prince, and a French lieutenant: our
o'clock dinner was a pleasant occasion, and the baroness
who 'wore a very sensible bonnet, coming well over the
head . . . allowed that even in the depth of winter in St.
Petersburg, the ladies are such slaves to fashion that they
wear the bonnets only on the backs of their heads leaving all
the top exposed to the intense cold.'

Conversation turned to the actions of the English fleet,
and Sulivan wrote

> you cannot imagine the impression that is gone against us;
> stories have been invented and exaggerated, and I believe
> many think us most brutal barbarians, who burn and
> destroy without mercy; but sometimes they have too much
> cause for thinking so . . . Count Stakleberg has a pretty
> villa and bathing house on the coast where he had his

whole family, with daughters and some visitors. One beautiful evening they were dining on the verandah and were looking at some of our vessels off there, and were remarking how pretty they looked . . . when one fired a shot at the house . . . followed by another. Can you wonder at their thinking us brutes? . . . The fact is there is a kind of unfeeling, senseless, anxiety to fire at anything that gives a chance, for the sake of firing, and some, I fear, for the sake of notoriety, or the chance of lying about the pretence of a fight so that they might write a letter.

Sulivan was scathing about those of his brother officers who wrote letters home describing minor actions in heroic terms, that were again magnified in local newspapers. 'I am afraid there are few of our men that can really be trusted in command, or are fit to decide on what should or should not be done. As to younger officers, I am sorry to say I see little signs of any prudence or judgment to prevent them doing any silly or disgraceful thing if they can only have a shot at something or try to get up a fight for the chance of getting their names mentioned.'

He was scathing, too, about honour and glory: 'there is great anxiety about the promotions which are expected tomorrow . . . I look more anxiously for some hopes of peace . . . I do hope there is a strong feeling leading all Christian churches at home to pray earnestly for peace and to check those feelings of fancied military honour and glory which lead so many to counsel and to wish for war. If they could feel a little of the horrors suffered by the poor people at Kertch and the misery and anxiety caused by driving people with their things from their homes in Helsingfors and Revel they would think very differently about the war.' He had been reading Wellington's despatches and wrote, 'it is singular how exactly he complains like us of the falsehood and injury of the newspaper articles. They were abusing him for doing nothing at the very time he had more difficulties to struggle with than ever . . . but no paper had the influence then with the public that *The Times* has now, and these attacks on us all are, of course, delightful to the enemy. We hear that *The Times* is received inside Sebastopol the day it reaches our camp and eagerly read for information about the army etc.'

Meanwhile, in the southern theatre of war, in May 1855, a few months before the bombardment of Seaborg, *Vesuvius* took part in the Kertch expedition, a modified fulfilment of a more grandiose scheme dreamed up by Napoleon III himself and accepted by his allies during his state visit to London. This was an attempt to throttle the supply lines to Sebastopol by capturing the harbour of Kertch on the east of the Crimean Peninsular. As Eupatoria to the north-west was also in allied hands, it was held that Sebastopol would be reduced to overland supplies through a very long line of communication if this attack could succeed. The expedition sailed on 4 May, the day after telegraphic communication was established by means of underwater cables, linking the Crimea with the outer world. The first message to be received was from Napoleon III himself, recalling the French ships to go to Constantinople to embark the French army of diversion waiting there. The expedition returned and three weeks later set sail again to achieve complete success. There were fifteen thousand infantry, French, Turkish, British, and five batteries of artillery embarked in a fleet of fifty-six sail. The force entered the strait on 24 May and landed at Kamish, where the Russians, taken by surprise, blew up the fortifications on both sides of the straits. Supplies for Sebastopol were destroyed and the shallow draught vessels went on into the sea of Azov to deal with the unarmed transports plying between Kertch and the Don ports.

Altogether one hundred vessels were destroyed before the main body of the expedition returned on 15 June, leaving a force of just two thousand troops to hold the positions. Captain Osborn of *Vesuvius* became senior officer of the ships remaining in the area.

However, these are only the bald outlines of the expedition. For more detail we must turn to the letters to the Admiralty of Rear-Admiral Sir Edmund Lyons. On 19 May he wrote to the Secretary of the Admiralty complaining that if only the Kertch expeditionary force had not been recalled the allies could have given great encouragement to the Circassians in revolt against Russian government. Lyons, who had earned a reputation as something of a fire-eater, criticized the enormous build-up of troops, including a reinforcement of thirty thousand French and Sardinians, far more than were required for the investing of Sebastopol, and a large fleet, much of it inactive, when the allies could make themselves masters of the Sea of Azov. He quoted a despatch from Commander Osborn, Sulivan's Captain in *Vesuvius* who said that the Turkish General at Chalanjih hoped to arrange a plan of combined operations with the Circassian chiefs against Russian ports still remaining on the Circassian seaboard, and that the General—Mustapha Pasha—had used the services of *Vesuvius* to make his reconnaissances. Meanwhile the enemy were reinforcing Kertch and blocking the deep water channel off Yenikale. In a later letter Commander Osborn said that Mustapha Pasha was convinced that, given proper assistance, there could be an invaluable Circassian rising, and that Circassian officers in Russian employ would turn against their masters.

On 26 May, Admiral Lyons wrote 'the allied forces are masters of the Straits of Kertch and that they have in the Sea of Azov a powerful steam flotilla of light draught of water, capable of cutting off the enemy's supplies and harassing him at all ports.' He went on to say that he and the French Admiral Bruat accompanied into the Sea of Azov a steam flotilla of fourteen British ships, (including *Vesuvius* and *Beagle*) and five French steamers.

Meanwhile the squadron was kept busy intercepting sailing vessels, chasing steamers, exchanging fire with cavalry and destroying guard houses, barracks and stores of forage and provisions.

In a letter of 17 July to Admiral Lyons, Commander Osborn described an attack on Fort Petrouski in which ten British and two French gun boats took part. The light draught boats took up stations east and west of the fort enfilading the works in front and rear, whilst the heavier vessels formed a semicircle round the fort which was first bombarded and then attacked by the light boats of the squadron which destroyed the batteries. The Crooked Spit in the Gulf of Azov was cleared of cavalry and Cossacks, and Sulivan was mentioned as being in charge of the ship's boats of *Vesuvius*. Reconnoitring the mouth of the river Mions guarded by Fort Temenos, *Vesuvius* and *Curlew* and the gun vessels *Cracker*, *Boxer* and *Jasper* encountered cavalry in large bodies, armed with carbines or rifles.

When they were directly underneath Fort Temenos, which stood on an eighty-foot cliff, they found themselves looked down upon by a large body of horse and foot, lining the ditch and parapet of the work. Landing on the opposite bank at good rifle shot distance, one boat's crew under Lieutenant Rowley was sent to destroy a collection of launches and a fishery, while a careful and steady fire of *minié* rifles kept the Russians from advancing.

Sulivan is also mentioned in a letter from Commander Cranford to Osborn. Addressed *Swallow*, off Crooked Spit, Sea of Azov, 15 July 1855, it describes another reconnaissance and destruction of a fishing station and nets. The country was swarming with Russian cavalry, who were driven off 'as far into the land as we could see from the masthead of the *Grinder*,' and the firing of stores on the upper part of the spit, 'including large fishing establishments, an enormous quantity of nets, haystacks and several large houses used as government stores . . .'

On 25 July Commander Osborn wrote from *Vesuvius* to the Admiral . . .

. . . I have fully succeeded in destroying by means of submarine explosions the four Russian steamers sunk in Berdiansk Bay, and as the enemy had from the houses of the western suburb of Berdiansk twice fired upon our people whilst peaceably and unguardedly employed I considered it right that such a dishonourable course from a town which had been spared under a plea of being defenceless, should be severely punished, and the more so as Berdiansk had been treated with unusual leniency upon the occasion of our former visits.

It is interesting to speculate what Bartholomew Sulivan would have thought of this.

On 10 August, Commander Osborn wrote describing a reconniassance the squadron made off the mouth of the Don, to discover the feasibility of an attack on Rostov, and once again *Vesuvius*, and Sulivan, was in the thick of things. In no more than four foot of water, the gigs of the paddle-boats and the gunboats were rowed through 'a sinuous channel' as far as a stockade which barred their way apart from a very narrow channel left for the Russians' own convenience, with earthworks mounting guns and a decked boat on either side. Beyond them stretched miles of green rushes and the marsh of the delta.

The bulrushes which fringed the whole delta like a screen were seen to be full of troops, who from their uniforms appeared to be riflemen; and numbers of rowing boats pulling six oars each moved out on either flank. The paddle-boats were anchored and the gigs, Sulivan with them, continued to advance until about eight hundred yards from the enemy's defences.

As at least two thousand Russians were seen in different places, Osborn decided against even a feint attack, 'as it would only give the enemy an opportunity of writing a despatch to announce a victory.'

Other letters from Commander Osborn describe similar incidents, of reconnaissances and landings in small boats, burning stores, and returning the fire from Russian riflemen. On 1 September he wrote to describe an incident ashore at the anchorage of Lyanpiria, where on one occasion he landed with the rocket boats of *Vesuvius* and *Wrangler*, and was ambushed by about fifty Russians who charged, shouting as they advanced, and managed to capture three sailors.

The next letter from Osborn, now a Captain, is a remarkable document, for it is the refutation by a British naval officer of allegations made not only by the British Consul still in post at Taganrog, but also by Count Tolstoi, then its Governor. Both the Consul, Mr Martin, and Tolstoi accused Osborn of unnecessary damage to civilian property and life, to which Osborn replied with a fierce defensiveness, and although his statements are plausible enough, one wonders what Bartholomew would have thought. Tolstoi had published a despatch in the *St Petersburgh Gazette* (apparently read by British Naval Officers),

> in which the first attack by the allied squadron upon Taganrog

wrote Osborn,

> was represented as a cruel and unnecessary act, whilst at the same time the Count claimed a victory, because the late Captain Edmund Lyons, our senior officer, was forbearing and merciful . . .
>
> I cannot conceive that any one out of Russia will believe that British naval officers are capable of such brutality as to fire at women and children, and therefore, unless you desire it, neither upon that head nor the equally gross charge of such acts being committed under the influence of noon-day potations, will I enter farther than to say it is a malicious falsehood.

Describing the action criticized by Mr Martin, Osborn wrote:

> Alone, with her one gun and small crew, that steamer did fully succeed in harassing the 'victorious' garrison of Taganrog, as well as its gallant Governor, and I dare say alarmed the inhabitants . . . Lieutenant Hudson I think did perfectly right in firing occasionally at the enemy's earthworks; he would have been much to blame had he allowed himself to be suddenly surprised by their opening fire upon him; the capture of all boats afloat was a judicious precaution to prevent being boarded at night by the enemy; and so far as injury to the hospital is concerned it is still standing, looking a little the worse for the stray shots that may have now and then hit it. But Count Tolstoi, as well as Mr. John Martin (the British Consul), must remember that a hospital which has an earthen rampart pierced with embrasures 100 yards in its rear, as well as an entrenchment parapet, and guns, within a few

feet of its front, is more likely to suffer from the fire of an enemy. Humanity would suggest that the sick had better be in a safer spot.

To the west of the hospital stands a long row of barracks; they are in every respect similar in appearance to the hospital, and from the gunboats' anchorage the whole of these buildings are in line . . . In short, sir, so far am I from believing that Taganrog has been too severely dealt with, that it is a source of regret to me that the loss of *Jasper*, and the defective state of *Clinker* and *Boxer*, rendered it impossible for me constantly to have such a force before the city as would have given the enemy little rest, and still further impeded the arming of the batteries.

After the wreck of *Jasper*, to which Captain Osborn referred, no diver or diving apparatus was available so George, who was a very powerful swimmer, volunteered to go down to see what he could save. He spent four days diving, sometimes submerged for as long as two minutes at a time, and recovered a sixty-eight pound gun from two fathoms of water. He also managed to get into the engine room and shut the valves, and into the magazine to find out if the Russians had cleared it of ammunition. Finally, after the surgeon had said that he was too exhausted to do any more, he insisted on finishing the job and placed powder casks under the vessel to blow her up. For this he was again mentioned in despatches.

The last major operations of the squadron were a series of actions ashore, with the object of destroying enemy stores.

The town of Glofire was attacked and the enemy were driven out of their trenches, a small brass cannon was captured, and the Russians driven from store to store, until the whole of a vast quantity of corn stacked ready for threshing and transport was in flames and burnt fiercely throughout the night. The gunboats anchored in their own draught of water, within long gunshot of the east extremity of Gheisk and the neighbouring steppe, along the edge of which, for four miles, corn and hay were stacked in large quantities, and close to the town were timber-yards and fish stores, which were all set alight.

'The zeal, good conduct, and gallantry of the men were deserving of every praise' wrote Osborn.

The squadron of steam vessels served in the Sea of Azov between the end of May and November and on their return the war was virtually over. The main events on land had been: the bombardment of 6 June in which five hundred and forty-five allied guns fired at targets in Sebastopol, and the bloody victory of the French who captured the Mamelon redoubt; the failure of the attack on the Redan and the great Russian fortification of the Malakov on 18 June (anniversary of Waterloo); the disastrous failure of the Russian counter-attack in the Tchenaye Valley on 16 August; the great three-day allied bombardment, beginning on 5 September, the French capture of the Malakoff on the 8th, the Russian engineering feat of constructing a pontoon bridge across the harbour which enabled them to evacuate the town on the evening of the 9th and the entry of the allies on the 10th; and finally a successful combined operation against Nikolinev at the mouth of the Dnieper. By now winter had set in, and with it military and political stalemate. In the early spring of the following year the war was over.

The log of *Vesuvius* is interesting for the more intimate details of war that it provides. There are entries that corroborate the broad outlines given in the despatches of her captain, but these are brief to the point of terseness:

7 June, observed fleet at anchor: 22 June, boats' crew fired at a party of Cossacks: 13 July, boarded Neapolitan and Austrian brigs: 20 September, observed the troops engaging the enemy: 27 September, sent boats to bring off wounded Russian prisoners: 14 October, landed field piece and party of seamen: 17 October, *Queen* weighed, Captain went on board same and steamed ahead and passed inside the line delivering broadsides against the Forts as they could be seen. 4.45 *Queen* took fire in two or three places, towed her out of action under a heavy fire, occasionally struck by shell.

Then, in 1855,

> 3 May, embarked nine officers and two hundred and sixty
> men of 83 Regiment: 24 May, at entrance to the lake at
> Kamisk, to cover landing of troops, tried range of big
> guns at a body of cavalry at 3,100 yards, fired at scattered
> parties of the enemy, paddle boats landed troops.

On 29 May, ninety vessels were destroyed by boats of the
squadron, on 5 June, the government stores in Taganrog
were destroyed, on 28 June ninety-one wagons laden with
salt were destroyed, on 22 July, the suburb of Bediansk
'whence our boats have lately been fired on' suffered a
similar fate.

Shipboard life continued in its many other aspects. Every
round fired in salute for a Turkish General who came aboard
had to be checked and accounted for, and so had the damage
done in the great bombardment of 17 October 1854, which
had particularly affected the wardroom: 'broken by shot
from Russian forts: decanters 1, tumblers 24, glasses sherry
6, port 5, claret 6, champagne 9 . . .' There are entries
'scrubbed and washed clothes,' 'employed in hoisting in
cattle and stock for the fleet,' 'coaling stations,' 'divine
service,' 'mustered at quarters,' 'landing cattle.'

There were disciplinary problems, and severe measures:
'punished James Metcalf 30 lashes for getting drunk whilst
on duty ashore at Yalta, disrated A. B. Maxwell, Captain of
the Forecastle, for insolence, insubordination, and mutinous
expressions.' Another received 24 lashes for 'skulking' as
well as insubordination, and a midshipman was reprimanded
for 'disobedience of orders, for being dirty at divisions and
for having his mess place in a disgraceful state.' A bosun,
2nd class, was placed under arrest for 'insolence and con-
temptuous conduct' and when sent for was again insolent,
and returned to his cabin. Finally he was released after
'having publicly acknowledged his misconduct and expressed
his contrition.'

Meanwhile, as always at sea, there were the elements to
contend with, and their danger was often greater than those
afforded by the enemy. In November 1854 there was a

tremendous storm: the entry is matter of fact but it does not stretch the imagination too far to glimpse the furies of the storm as endured in a small gun vessel. 'Heavy squalls came on from the southward, sent top gallant masts on deck. 9.30 struck lower yards and top masts . . . 9.50 wind increased to a perfect hurricane, let go sheet anchor . . . 10.30 cut away mizzen mast . . . main mast went by the board.' Later they had to throw three guns over board and the ship had to be kept broadside to the swell rolling heavily. No wonder the entries for the next few days read 'cleaning ship, drying sails and clearing out holds.'

The men of *Vesuvius*, and of the fleet in general, may not have endured the same desperate hardships as the wretched ill-equipped soldiers during the first winter in the Crimea which Russell of *The Times*, the photographer Fenton, Miss Nightingale and others were to publicize to good cause at home; but they too had their hardships and they too earned their Crimean medals—those that survived.

The war came to its inconclusive end in 1855. The following year peace was made, and in 1857 Bartholomew in *Merlin* led one of the two divisions at the Queen's review of the Baltic Fleet, the year in which old Admiral Thomas Ball Sulivan died.

Bartholomew was one of the Commissioners involved in the trial of a 'submarine boat' in Poole harbour and the next year he became 'Professional Officer' to the Board of Trade, where he served for eight years and in which he was concerned with the 'lights boards of the United Kingdom . . . and the departments of lights, pilotage and lifeboats.' For the first four years the Bartholomew Sulivans lived at Isleworth, where he used to spend his Sunday afternoons in the poorer districts, distributing copies of 'The British Workman,' which he would sometimes read aloud to groups of people. One day when he was visiting the brick fields a woman said to him 'its all very well for you to tell us not to drink beer and then go home to your glass of wine,' and this so affected him that he never again took a glass.

In summer they would return to the family home at Flushing, Falmouth, where his mother still lived and where

Bartholomew Sulivan and his sons spent much of their time afloat in small craft. The *Philomel*, in which he had served up the Parana, was at one time moored as a hulk in the harbour, and on her deck he would retell the story of Obligado to his family.

In 1863 he went on to the reserve list of Admirals and two years later gave up the house which he had planned for himself and had had built at Roehampton, and retired to Bournemouth.

After the war George served in *Ajax* and *Exmouth* before returning once again to the Royal Yacht, *Victoria and Albert*, and in 1862 was promoted Commander. Whilst serving in *Exmouth* at Suda Bay on 6 October 1860, he saw a seaman, Thomas Burke, fall overboard. He dived in from the poop, a height of thirty feet from the water, and was so long submerged that the ship's company thought he had drowned. At last he surfaced, holding Burke in his right hand. His commanding officer wrote, 'He hit the exact angle . . . about 20 feet down.' The next day the petty officers came aft 'to express, in the name of the crew, their thanks . . .'

The logbooks of *Victoria and Albert*, unlike those of the other ships in which he served, do not provide much to stimulate the imagination. For most of the year she was in home waters, and the entries are confined to remarks such as 'sent boys to church,' and 'seamen practised cutlass drill;' there was a great deal of painting and furbishing and the usual maintenance of sails, but very few disciplinary problems. Between June and August there was much coming and going of Royalty, with entries such as 'Prince and Princess Louis of Hesse embarked, Prince and Princess Louis disembarked accompanied by the Duke de Brabant in the Belgian State Barge, Prince of Wales and Prince Arthur embarked, Her Majesty and the Princesses Helena, Louise and Beatrice and suite embarked from *Fairy*, Princess Hohenlohe accompanying Her Majesty.' There were short summer cruises, especially to the Belgian coast 'anchored off Antwerp, Her Majesty disembarked in the barge of the King of the Belgians.'

Sulivan would have been introduced to Her Majesty and to accompanying Royalty, and this period of service in home waters may have been a welcome and interesting change, followed as it was by a spell with HM Coastguard. The Coastguard service had been reorganized by act of Parliament only two years before, and had been transferred to the Admiralty, partly in order to furnish a reserve force of seamen. By this time most of the officers and two thirds of the men in the coastguard were sailors who had served several years afloat, but were liable for recall, and the change was dictated by the need to ensure that greater efficiency was reached in their reserve training, impossible under the former customs organization.

Men-of-war were stationed at all the principal ports to act as Headquarters of local coastguard sections, with the existing revenue cruisers augmented by some of the small twin screw gun boats from the Sea of Azov. At Falmouth in 1857 the Headquarters ship was *Eagle*, a seventy-four-gun ship built in 1804, whose area extended from Plymouth to the Bristol Channel, under command of a captain with several divisions under him, each under an inspecting commander, of whom Sulivan was one. In addition to the sailors in his command, George Sulivan now found himself responsible for soldiers, as each coastguard station continued to have a mounted guard, as in the old service, whose members were drawn from cavalry regiments, and whose duties were to patrol the lanes at night to search out smugglers' haunts and rendezvous. The sailors of the service had multifarious duties ashore, but they also included a great deal of boat work, under oars and sails as well as armed sea training; and in his native Falmouth waters, where he had learnt to row and to sail as a boy, no doubt George was happy to exercise his coastguard men in the ways of small boats and seamanship.

It was during this time that he performed another act of bravery, to earn him once again the commendation of the Royal Humane Society. It was a still and starlit evening in June 1863. He was standing at the top of his mother's steep garden at Flushing near Falmouth when he heard the creak of oars in a boat followed by a splash, and a cry for help, and then silence. He sprinted the two-hundred-and-fifty yards to the quay where he was able to step straight into a boat as the tide was high. He and a waterman each took an oar and were directed by two other men at the quay who had some idea of where the man had gone down. One of these who helped Sulivan strip his shirt off before diving in, said to him 'Your father saved my life off this very spot fifty years ago,' and indeed, Sulivan's elder brother Bartholomew remembered their father jump in and swim ashore with a child under his arm. That child was now the man on the quay. Sulivan dived in a number of times and at last located the man—a navvy who had hired a boat—but he was already dead.

CHAPTER 4

RETURN TO AFRICA

George Sulivan at the age of thirty-four was now set into his mould, firmly convinced of the righteousness of his religious principles as a result of upbringing and precept and deeply influenced by his brother's views on the evils of war. He himself had been through his baptism of fire and was no longer the larking midshipman from the days with *Castor*'s boats. He was a good seaman, a just captain, personally brave, and now at the height of his powers he was once again to encounter the slave trade, in his opposition to which he was to make no concessions to pragmatism or expediency.

On 11 May 1866 he sailed for Aden in the P & O Mail Steamer *Syris*, and as the Suez Canal was not yet finished the passengers went overland to Suez where he found the new hotel to be a fascinating sight!

> There were men and women from Hong Kong, from Shanghai, from Australia, Calcutta and Bombay; there were Chinese, Japanese, Turks and Parsees and representatives of almost every nation, European, Asiatic, African and American. There were invalid sailors and invalid soldiers; there were fresh looking Englishmen going abroad, and sallow faced ones coming home; some there were who had never been home for half their life time and some going out probably never to return.

On 3 June they reached Aden, and an hour or two later *Pantaloon* rounded the point and anchored, and Sulivan took over his first command. She was a steam sloop of five hundred and seventy-four tons, screw propelled, capable of one hundred and fifty hp, carrying eleven guns. She had an officer complement of two lieutenants, a master, a surgeon and his assistant, a paymaster and his assistant, and two sub-

lieutenants, and was one of the seven ships on the East
Indies station under Captain Hillyer. She had recently, under
the command of Captain Purvis, liberated three hundred
slaves, including fifty Galla women intended for the harem
of the Imam of Muscat.

Much of the subsequent voyage was described by Sulivan
in his book, but as it was specifically written to portray the
slave trade, most of the routine naval life was omitted. For
every day engaged in hunting slaves there were many others
when the normal round of shipboard life at sea and ashore
was unbroken by any contact with the slave trade. There
were storms to contend with, and Admiralty instructions to
be heeded with regard to a hundred-and-one details of
commissariat, supply and trading. Entries such as these
occur frequently in the ship's log: 'exercised at general
quarters, sailmakers making spare foresail, making and
mending clothes, divisions, weighed under steam, drew fire
and blew out boilers, exchanged longitudes with English
barque *Maria*, cleaning ship after coaling, painting ship's
sides.' There are frequent references to cutlass, rifle and gun
drill, and occasional disciplinary troubles: 'Commander
severely reprimanded Mr. H. G. Hatch (master's assistant)
for neglect of duty'—but on the whole *Pantaloon* seems to
have been a happy ship, as she ploughed her way to the
Seychelles, Zanzibar, Pemba, Mohilla, the Cape, Trincomalee, Mauritius, Simons Bay, St Helena, Ascension,
Sierra Leone; sometimes under steam, more often under sail,
butting in the teeth of the monsoon and tropical storms.
However, all this was ahead when Sulivan went aboard his
first command.

He was glad to leave Aden, 'the most abominable hole in
existence,' and was delighted to sail down the gulf, with the
thermometer falling to eighty-five degrees, and to greet the
sight of dhows whose 'huge sails, lofty sterns and low bows
give them the appearance of some great sea monster in the
act of diving; they recalled much of those boat-cruising days
long ago and of many a pleasant incident connected with
them, which made me look upon them as if they were old
friends . . .'

On June 27, they anchored in Port Victoria at Mahé, in the Seychelles, which Sulivan described as 'an exceedingly picturesque island, being richly covered with verdure, coconut and other palm trees. It is celebrated for the coco-de-mer tree, which is indigenous to this place only . . . This tree received its name through a mistake on the part of some French officers, who, picking up one of the large nuts at sea, never having seen it before, and discovering it to be an unknown fruit, came to the conclusion that it grew in the sea, and gave it the name of "coco-de-mer".'

At Zanzibar, Sulivan met Dr Kirk*—who was to be the great architect of the suppression of slavery—'in whose society I have since spent many pleasant hours, and have witnessed, to some extent, his anxious endeavours and indefatigable exertions in all matters relating to the celebrated African explorer, Dr. Livingstone' (whom he had accompanied up the Zambesi on the launch *Ma Robert*) 'nor must I forget to mention our friend, Bishop Tozer, who every Sunday when we were at Zanzibar, made the ship his cathedral and who was always too good not to remember that if half his congregation were churchmen, the other half were dissenters . . .'

When Sulivan returned to Zanzibar fifteen years after his first tour of duty in East African waters, he found a harbour crowded with dhows of all sizes. Both at the beginning and at the end of the south-west monsoon before it reached its strength or when it had declined, the numbers increased considerably as preparations were made, for the voyage to the north, and between September and November there were daily sailings to the Red Sea, the Arabian coast, Muscat, the Persian Gulf and India. There were also larger merchant vessels of which there were more German than British, a few French and an occasional American. The town itself had a white population of between sixty and seventy people, including women and children, of whom about a

*Sir John Kirk, b. 1843, botanist on Livingstone's Zambesi voyage, subsequently surgeon, then Consul and Consul-General in Zanzibar, and architect of the Great Treaty of 1873 abolishing the slave trade within the Sultan's dominions: died 1922.

third were British, a third French and the rest German and American. Over two-thirds were missionaries. There were a few hundred Hindu merchants, considerably more Muslims, several thousand Africans of the original indigenous tribes, about twenty thousand slaves who did the manual labour on the clove plantations, and of course, the Arabs. The town stood on a three-sided spit of land between the sea and a shallow creek whose beach was the repository for refuse and the main cause of the semi-permanent smell which hung over the place. The town itself was a maze of narrow streets, in which the huge brass studded wooden doors of merchants' houses gave no glimpse of the life which revolved within around internal courtyards. There were also a few larger flat-topped whitewashed houses, some mosques, the Sultan's Palace, narrow bazaars, unmade roads with huge evil-smelling black puddles—and the slave market.

At this time the trade was still legal from Kilwa Kivinge, two hundred miles south of Zanzibar, to Lamu, two hundred and thirty miles north. Although the clause in the existing treaty nominally limited the number of slaves to be carried to the Sultan's requirements for the clove plantations, he alone was the judge of these needs. Consequently, traders had only to pay their tax and apply for a licence which was granted without difficulty. Any vessel possessing such licence was exempt from detention and capture by British warships. Even if vessels arrived at Zanzibar with a number of slaves in excess of those specified in its papers, the Navy could not board them without the special permission of the Sultan himself, which he never gave unless to meet his own interests against those of the northern Arabs. Sulivan was incensed to see that dhows full of slaves could be anchored in Zanzibar harbour 'in such numbers as to surround the English flag carried by our cruisers, who cannot touch them.' He compared this unfavourably with the China seas, where the crews of maurauding junks were called pirates and executed; 'yet this infinitely worse piracy is covered by a treaty on the part of a despicable petty Arab chief, who, if we withdrew our protection would be murdered the next day, and his territory transferred to another; unless, indeed, some other European nation than the English should step in, and, without the same sentimental respect for territory possessed and governed by those through whom it is made a curse to all mankind, civilized and uncivilized, take possession of it themselves, and who, perhaps, having no such pure intention towards the negro as to be of any benefit to them, afterwards might simply carry on a limited slave-trade under another name.'*

Sulivan's strictures were not confined to Arabs, for he was equally critical of the French and Portuguese, especially the latter who 'not only enslave their bodies, but place moral chains and fetters for centuries to come on their whole mental being.' There is more than a whiff of anti-catholic dissent in his attitude to the Portuguese. 'It is frightful to contemplate beings so little raised above the brute creation, in a place which has been in possession of Christians, so called, for hundreds of years.'

He saw several slave dhows in Zanzibar harbour laden with slaves. 'The poor creatures are stowed sometimes in two, sometimes in three tiers on extemporized bamboo decks, not sufficiently distant from each other to allow them to sit upright.' Their licence took them as far as Lamu, the limit of the Sultan's territory, and as any dhow going farther towards the Arabian Coast or Persian Gulf, went at her own risk, the Captains took in as many slaves as possible after sending out scouts to pry out the movements of British warships. They would sail northward, keeping close to the land, with the intention of running their vessels on shore if chased, and also of putting in at the various small ports on the way to obtain a handful of rice and a cup of water per slave on board, and to fill up the gaps in the cargo caused by death. This was the illegal extension, and consequent result of having a legal slave-trade. A large number of these dhows obtained their cargoes far south of the southern limit Quiloa, from Quelimane, Angoxa, Mozambique, Ibo, the Por-

---

*Sulivan's intemperate remarks about the Sultan were not shared by Kirk who grew to respect the ruler of a kingdom whose economy had always been based on slavery but who ultimately conceded the expediency of abolishing the trade which supplied the raw material.

tuguese possessions on the coast, calling only at Quiloa to obtain the necessary pass for all of them, by possibly paying only a tax to the Custom House there for a few more to be added to their cargo at that place.

Sulivan considered that the 'slave-trade in Portuguese territory had actually increased, despite treaties to which Portugal was a party.'

One morning at Zanzibar, he went on deck with his interpreter, Jumah, just in time to see a huge dhow pass under their stern; her upper bamboo deck so covered with slaves squatting there, that not a square foot of it was visible. As she passed, every face on board her was turned towards the British ship, and the Arabs from the raised deck or poop abaft, gave a derisive cheer followed by laughter. One of them, seeing Jumah, hailed him.

'"What does he say, Jumah," I asked.

'"He say, ah! why you not come and take us, are you afraid?"

'Jumah replied: "We catch you another time."'

'"I got lots of slaves on board, tell the captain to come and see."'

This was followed by raucous laughter, as she passed into the harbour, lowered her sail, and anchored within pistolshot of Sulivan.

After a visit to the Sultan and 'a consummate caricature of royal pomp witnessed'—for Sulivan was not a man for half measures when he felt moral disapproval—*Pantaloon* sailed from Zanzibar and anchored off Pemba island where the boats were despatched to examine the harbours and creeks in order to ascertain if there were any vessels with unlicensed slaves on board, landing Jumah at the town to obtain information from his friends.

From Pemba they sailed to the Commoro group and anchored off the picturesque island of Mohilla. On 20 August some of the crew went ashore to pay their respects to the ruling Queen. Sulivan and Mr Shapcote, the paymaster, ascended a hill in company with three Arab chiefs who they assumed to be prime minister, foreign secretary, and commander-in-chief of 'all the forces,' which consisted of twenty-five to thirty men of various shades, who were ordered by the commander-in-chief to halt and shoulder arms in English—the only words in that language that they knew. They were dressed in scarlet tailcoats, probably bought in India from British soldiers twenty years before, and some even had the mitre hats, and oilskin caps of the Peninsular war, and were armed with flintlock muskets. Escorted by this force, Sulivan was borne in a contraption 'formed of the bottoms of old chairs screwed to two oars with the blades cut off' to the residence of the Queen, who was seated on a dais in an inner room, swathed so that only her eyes were visible.

Not long after this, *Pantaloon* sailed for the Cape and thence, via Zanzibar and the Seychelles to Trincomalee in Ceylon, and very shortly afterwards returned to England, paying off at Plymouth on 6 March 1867, the latest entry in the log being 'sunset—hauled down the pennant.'

Four months later Sulivan was appointed to command *Daphne*, like *Pantaloon* also a sloop, but considerably larger, 1081 tons, and with a screw engine capable of three-hundred hp. She had been built the precceeding year, and he commissioned her for service on the East Indian station.

The first entry in *Daphne*'s log reads 'Thursday 12 June 1867 at Devonport, 10 a.m. Commander G. L. Sulivan commissioned the ship. Mr. George White, master, joined' followed the next day by Lieutenant Gardner and Mr Bascombe, clerk. On 17 June, three tons of water were taken aboard, and also the nucleus of the crew. There were seventeen men from *Indus*, twelve from *Cambridge*, twenty-four from *Canopus,* seven from *June*, one from *Liverpool*, and seventeen marines from barracks—all these differing strands had to be welded into a composite whole to form a crew with an allegiance to their new ship. On the 19th, they 'dressed ship in honour of the Queen's accession,' and again on the 28th to commemorate her Coronation day; on the 23rd for the first time they mustered for divisions, and the next day was occupied in bending and storing sails, and before the end of the month they received on board forty-three rifles, thirteen pistols, fifty swords, one six pound gun and one hundred and fifty shot. On the 25th June they were coaling and bending small sails.

Some entries for July read

issued rifles, read fire drill and stationed ship's company at fire quarters, running measured mile . . . Richard Osborne (stoker) died from injuries received from a bag of coals falling on his head . . . 7 July lighted fires under three boilers, weighed and proceeded out of the Sound under steam . . . 12 July anchored at Spithead . . . The Royal Yacht *Victoria and Albert* with Her Majesty Queen Victoria on board passed through the fleet on her way to Osborne . . . 17 July the royal Yacht *Victoria and Albert* with Her Majesty Queen Victoria, His Imperial Turkish Majesty the Sultan and His Imperial Highness the Viceroy of Egypt followed by two other Royal Yachts and P. and O. ships with the Lords and Commons, H.M. Ships *Terrible* and *Gladiator*, passed down the line from Osborne. The ships manning rigging, cheering and firing Royal Salutes in honour of Their Majesties . . . 30 July weighed under steam for trial under the measured mile. Admiral Wellesley and dockyard officials came on board to conduct trials.

In August they sailed to Plymouth, then back to Devonport, and at last on 19 August they set sail, arriving after a smooth passage on 5 September, at Sierra Leone. From there they went on to Ascension and the Cape of Good Hope. There are the usual routine shipboard entries: 'young gentlemen at rifle drill, issued soap and tobacco to ship's company, scrubbed canvas gear.' The weather got warmer, the winds lighter and the skies bluer, but approaching the Cape they hit a heavy squall, with Force six winds, rising to Force seven. There was a heavy list of damage entered in the log (reminiscent of *Vesuvius* many years before in the Sea of Azov): as on that occasion, decanters and champagne glasses seem to have been particularly vulnerable, as well as liqueur glasses, cups and saucers, pie dishes, egg cups, breakfast and dinner plates and many other articles.

On 14 October, they anchored off Simonstown, from

whence they sailed to Mauritius, and across the Indian Ocean, the sea temperature now rising to the mid-eighties. Winds were light and most of this passage was under steam, unlike the passage out to the Cape.

Sulivan described a tragic incident that occurred during this voyage across the Indian Ocean which gives us a vivid insight not only into his own character but also the appalling decisions that had to be made by Captains in the days of sail.

. . . after leaving the Cape, running to the eastward before a severe gale, the wind on the starboard quarter, under close-reefed main-topsail and reefed foresail, topmast-staysail and storm main-trysail, a heavy sea struck the ship on the starboard beam, knocking in the upper-deck iron ports and waist netting, lifting the end of the bridge on which Sub-Lieutenant Orton was standing as officer of the watch, and washed him overboard. The sea had so covered the deck, and poured down the hatchway also, that for a minute or two no one missed him. He who should have been on the alert for such an occurrence, and have acted in the event of such an accident, was himself the victim.

'Two minutes, or perhaps more, elapsed before those on board missed the officer of the watch from the bridge, or suspected its cause—a lapse of time that may be estimated by the fact that the first lieutenant had just reached my cabin to report that the lower deck was covered with water, and to ask if he should batten down, when the boatswain's mate ran aft to report the officer of the watch overboard. The ship was brought to the wind, and life-buoys let go, but poor Orton could be seen swimming half-a-mile astern. It was already late in the evening, and dusk; the fires were lighted ith the view of using steam if possible, but it could not be up for nearly two hours. It was a question of minutes with the poor fellow, and it blew too hard to allow of the boats being lowered.

'I know of no more painful position to be placed in than that of the commander of a ship under such circumstances,—with volunteers around him begging to be allowed to go away in the lifeboat to rescue a shipmate, perhaps a messmate, and who, though they do not see it, are ready to leave the responsibility of their lives in their commander's hands, without considering the consequences—to be compelled to come to the decision that the powerful swimmer must sink, knowing that to lower a boat would be certain death to many more. It was the second time that I had been so painfully situated, once in the *Pantaloon* and now again in the *Daphne*. It was now dark, and blowing harder than ever, and with sadder feelings that I can express, I left the deck, giving orders that the ship should be steered her course again.'

Routine continued: always making and mending, exchanging colours with other ships, and occasional odd entries such as 'hammock lost overboard by accident:' and in addition to divine service on Sundays the Captain sometimes read prayers in the middle of the week. On 19 November they reached Bombay where the dockyard artificers caulked the ship, and the crew painted her sides, coaled ship, cleaned ship, washed clothes, fitted the cutter's falls, assisted in putting a fire out on a merchant ship, and endured many other chores.

They sailed, under steam, on 30 December, for Aden, and thence to Annesley Bay, on the Red Sea, in which area they spent most of the next six months.

Some years before this, the Emperor Theodore II of Ethiopia, had viewed with alarm the apparent encroachments of Muslims around his Christian state, and had thought that the British were supporting the Khedive of Egypt in this attempt. Ethipia had indeed been menaced by hostile Muslims for centuries, not only by Egyptians and Sudanese to the north and west, but also by Arabs in the south, who captured Christian slaves and transported them across the Red Sea to the Near East. Theodore therefore had some justification for his fears, and the British Consul, Captain Cameron did not appear to do much to allay them. When Theodore's letters to Queen Victoria remained unanswered, he imprisoned sixty-seven Europeans, including Cameron, in Magdala; General Sir Robert Napier and an army from India were despatched to rescue the captives.

Napier conducted an able campaign, with twelve thousand troops (the first campaign in which British soldiers had the new breech-loading Snider rifle), whom he had to move three hundred and eighty miles over practically unknown and difficult country, utilizing mules, camels and elephants for supply. They defeated Theodore's forces and advanced on Magdala, after Cameron and many of the Europeans had already been released. Theodore killed himself, and his body was found on the heights of Magdala.

The naval contribution consisted of eighty men with twelve rocket tubes commanded by Captain Fellowes of *Dryad*. Sulivan himself has left no indication as to whether he accompanied the land forces. It would certainly have been in keeping with his character to have had at least a brief excursion ashore. Clements Markham, who wrote *'The History of the Abyssinian Expedition'* in the following year wrote 'The Blue Jackets were, beyond dispute, the élite of the force. Always merry and cheerful, treating their mules kindly and loading them in a workmanlike manner, they went merrily over the marches and passed their evenings in singing.' The sailors went into action with their rockets at the Arogye Plain, when the Abyssinians, ensconced at the crest of the Fahla, poured down the slopes, their chiefs mounted on Galla ponies. That night, after a magnificent display of courage, the Abyssinians withdrew, and again the next day the sailors fired at the main body, until ordered to stop, a premature order that gave a very brief reprieve.

Daphne remained in Annesley Bay until 18 June 1868, when the troops were re-embarked, and a month later 'after escaping the south-west monsoon in all its strength,' reached Mahé, with the loss of their main yard. Log entries for the period in Annesley Bay are mostly routine, but on one occasion they had to slip the tow of a transport because of boiler trouble and 'the high wind (Force five) and sea' and they had to pump ship. In Annesley Bay itself there was coaling, cleaning, painting, working parties ashore, repairing of boats and the midshipmen being exercised at gun drill and the usual small incidents—'lost overboard by accident crutches metal.' Discipline was preserved and the

Captain 'reprimanded Mr. Harding, gunner, for not passing orders to his relief, when officer of the watch.'

On 6 August, *Daphne* arrived in the Seychelles and on the first Sunday the Catholics were despatched to chapel, as the French had established a Catholic mission, and Sulivan 'performed divine service' on board. By midweek more secular activities had taken place, and Mr Richards, carpenter, was placed under arrest, drunk and incapable of superintending the working party of artificers on shore.

Having obtained a new main yard from *Octavia* whose mainsail was the right size, *Daphne* sailed on to Tamatave where Sulivan obtained much useful information about the Madagascan slave trade from Mr Pakenham, the British Consul, who told him that by a treaty with the Queen of Madagascar, the traffic in slaves to that country had officially been abolished, but slavery still existed as a legal institution within the island.

Sulivan was impressed by the British Consul at Madagascar, who had been able to compel the authorities to fulfil the treaty whenever he heard of slaves being landed, and to insist on punishment of the trader and the surrender of the slaves to the British. Nevertheless, detection was comparatively rare, and the trade was very extensive, carried on chiefly from the Portuguese territory, sometimes direct, and sometimes through the Commoro Islands. Slaves were often taken to those islands via the French settlement at Nos Beh, under the French flag, and with the designation of 'passengers' or '*engagés.*'

On 9 September, *Pantaloon* left Tamatave and sailed to the north-west end of the island where, after examining that part of the coast, she steered for Mayotte, and anchored on the 17th off the town, inside the extensive coral reefs that formed the harbour.

Mayotte is one of the Commoro group, which consists of the four islands, Commoro, Johanna, Mayotte and Mohilla. At that time it was the only one to be governed by the French, the others still having their own rulers.

Sulivan, like a number of other naval officers, was impatient at the practice of diplomacy in dealing with local potentates, and was a man of his time in his assumption of superiority based on unquestioning moral certainty that people would be better off under enlightened British and Christian rule. Sometimes he failed to recognize the good qualities of rulers like Barghash and the difficulties with which he was faced, and on some occasions he was less than fair to other nations. According to him the French just hoisted their flag at Mayotte and took it over, whereas in fact Sultan Amadi agreed to a Treaty in 1841 with Lieutenant Jehenne of the French Navy by which he ceded his sovereign rights to France in return for a pension of five thousand francs a year, together with free education for his children.

From Mayotte, *Daphne* sailed to Johanna, where Sulivan compared 'the miserable filthy hovels' of the town unfavourably with the beautiful and fertile surrounding country which was covered with palm and coconut trees and 'abounded in pineapples, bananas, sweet potatoes and arrowroot etc.'

From there they sailed on to Mohilla, where he found that great changes had taken place since his first visit in *Pantaloon* two years previously. According to him, the French had acquired the island by typical French chicanery, although the story—of the award of rights, subsequently not honoured, and ultimately reinforced by gunboat pressure— may not have been so very different from some British activities. According to Sulivan, the gunboat commander even forced an entrance in the Queen's chamber, 'where she at the time was in *"dishabille,"* (*sic*), and for so doing, was very properly kicked out of the house,' thereupon the gunboat and another French vessel opened fire on the defenceless island, without further warning, killing several people, and then landed a force and took possession of the fort (as it was called, but without any guns in it). The Queen escaped from the island to Zanzibar, and thence proceeded to France, to lay her complaint before the Emperor,* 'who probably would have more sympathy with her now than at that time, as she gained little satisfaction.'

*The Emperor Napoleon III: before his exile in England.

It was soon after this occurrence that Sulivan arrived in *Daphne*. French troops had been landed from Mayotte, and the Frenchman—the author of the trouble—was now the young king's guardian. Consequently, Sulivan's party was treated with some reserve although the Guard of Honour wore the same elderly uniforms and were armed with the same ancient firelocks. In addition to these, however, there was a train of about one hundred Arabs who formed two lines between which he walked from the entrance to a seat on the right of the throne, which looked like an old armchair, placed on a deal table with half of each leg cut off. On this sat the handsome boy-king. Conversation, however, proved abortive, as no one would respond to Sulivan's attempt, through his interpreter, to probe their feelings towards the French. After a few minutes of this, he left the fort and returned to the ship.

Daphne continued her cruise to Mozambique and thence to Zanzibar by way of the Ruvuma river where they sighted and chased a dhow, which ran into the river and anchored close to some mangrove trees near the entrance. The chase was continued in the ship's boats and the dhow was boarded. There was no sign of any crew, only four slaves. From the filthy state of the vessel inside, there could be no doubt however that a cargo of slaves had just been landed. The next morning a similar dhow was chased and found to be completely deserted. But the most exciting part of the cruise was yet to come.

Arriving at Zanzibar on 12 October, they found the harbour crowded with dhows of every kind including several full of slaves, nominally bound for Lamu, but from reliable information received on *Daphne*, Sulivan had no doubt that several of them were determined to run the gauntlet along the coast. There were two reasons for this: slaves in such quantities were not required there, and a current war between tribes north of the Juba river was making the overland route too difficult, as they could no longer be marched to Brava, Magadoxa and places farther north, and then re-shipped for the Persian Gulf. Transport the whole way by sea was the only alternative.

Sulivan encouraged everyone to believe that his orders on leaving Zanzibar were to proceed to Bombay without mentioning that he intended to examine the coast to the north. He even undertook to carry freight for some Hindu merchants to Bombay, whom he suspected had only made the request in order to sound out his movements. He received a good deal of information about the legal traders in the harbour, and concluded, from past experience, that there would be no fittings in the unlicensed dhows that could be relied on as evidence, and even in the legal traders there would probably only be the unmistakable bamboo deck. His normal rule by now was never to detain any vessel except northern ones, from the sole evidence of having slave fittings, but to concentrate on those actually having slaves on board.

On the 21st, *Daphne* left Zanzibar under steam, heading for the north channel towards Bombay until clear of observation from the shore, and then altered direction to a course parallel to and thirty miles off the coast until they passed the latitude of Lamu when they sailed close into the shore and anchored on the night of the 24th off Brava. The following afternoon they chased and boarded a dhow which was a Zanzibar vessel with a number of domestic slaves, some of whom were in the service of one of the Sultan's sisters who was on board. The next day they boarded a legal trader which contained, in addition to domestic slaves, two boys who, the *Nakhoda* agreed, had been kidnapped at Pemba on the day of sailing. The dhow was subsequently 'condemned' at Zanzibar, the verdict being approved by the Sultan.

A few days later, a dhow was sighted coming from the south, so *Daphne* immediately weighed and steamed towards her. Suddenly, close in to the shore, she put her helm up and ran through the breakers on to the beach, becoming a complete wreck in a few minutes. By then *Daphne* was close to her, though still outside the breakers, and in time to see a crowd of unfortunate slaves struggling through the water from the ship to the shore. Many of them were probably drowned in the attempt, and others escaped up the hill, but Sulivan took a calculated risk to launch a boat to see if any

could be saved. They lowered a five-oared lifeboat, and together with a midshipman and the ship's carpenter, he
slipped down the lifelines until the boat had shoved off, intending, if the bar appeared too dangerous to cross, not to
risk the lives of the crew. The reef did not look so bad from
the outside, but suddenly, just as they caught sight of many of
the slaves on the beach and struggling in the water, they
found themselves amongst the breakers. A sea struck the lifeboat abaft, and washed clean over her from stem to stern,
and she would have broached-to if it had not been for the
weight of two of them on the yoke line. Another sea struck,
and then another, washing over the whole length of the boat
and everyone in it; but owing to her sturdy construction, the
seas went out over the bows, leaving only a few inches of
water in her. In a few minutes they were over the bar, and inside it was comparatively smooth, but Sulivan wondered how
they would ever get out for he had never seen such breakers,
and resolved never to cross them again. Once on land, they
found they were too late to rescue many of the slaves; however, they discovered seven little children from five to eight
years of age, who were too weak to crawl away into the bush.
One or two of them were doubled up with their knees against
their faces, in the position they had been in for many days,
and they were a week on board *Daphne* before they could
stretch out their legs. There was also a woman who had been
unable to save her child. She came down to the boat, but
while they were getting the children into it she disappeared.
They were above to shove off, when about twenty Somalis
came down waving spears and firelocks. Sulivan fired a rifle
at the ground about twenty yards ahead of them, which
stopped them advancing any further. By then it was nearly
dark, and twice they attempted in vain to cross the bar, each
time being carried back by the breakers. At last there appeared to be a lull in the furious surge of thundering foam;
the crew gave way with a will, and they succeeded in crossing,
getting only one heavy breaker over them from stem to stern,
the boat going through it like a fish.

On board *Daphne* the children told the interpreter that the
dhow had been crammed with slaves, but that on seeing the

ship the Arabs had told them, pointing to the smoke from the funnel, that the white man was lighting a fire to cook them with, and by this they persuaded the poor creatures to risk jumping into the water when they grounded.

On the 29th they chased a full slaver on shore in the same way. The moment the Arabs saw the ship, they steered the dhow through the breakers, and several hundred Africans could be seen landing. *Daphne*'s boats were able to land clear of the surf, but only rescued one male slave, who was in such a wretched condition that he could not crawl from the beach. He said that there were one hundred·and nineteen in the dhow and that some of them, in the same state as himself, were carried up the hill by other slaves.

On the 30th, another dhow full of slaves ran on shore and landed them at a time when *Daphne* had only one of the five boats available, as one cutter was detached on the coast, the whaler had just boarded a dhow some distance off, the gig was in chase of another, and the little dinghy was made fast to a dhow in charge of a prize crew. The remaining cutter, under charge of Lieutenant Acklom, was sent to chase this dhow, to endeavour to cut off and capture some of the escaping Arabs and negroes, as well as to overhaul the dhow on shore. Although no breakers were on this part of the coast, there was a heavy surf on the beach, and while the crew, after ineffectually chasing the runaways, were launching their boat in the surf, she was swamped, everything washed out of her, and in spite of every effort of those on shore, there seemed to be no prospect of their being able to get her head out and clear of the surf. *Daphne* was then about half-a-mile off the beach without another boat to assist the cutter, and there was no possibility of sending a line the necessary distance using the signal rocket. At last, the gig answered her recall, and returned in time to render assistance; the line was taken to the cutter, which was towed out of the surf, everyone in her drenched and exhausted.

As a result of these experiences, Sulivan conceived a plan to prevent the next slaver they encountered from running on shore by placing a boat inshore of them, and such a distance south of *Daphne* that the dhow would arrive abreast of her before she saw either the ship or boat; the coast was generally so straight, and the dhows sailed so close in, that they could escape unless the boat were concealed. This plan could therefore only be carried out about three miles south of Brava, where there was a coral rock projecting about twenty or thirty yards from the shore, forming a breakwater, stretching out beyond the breakers. Sulivan therefore made for this point, to the north of which he left the two cutters where they could not be seen from any dhow until it was abreast of them, and *Daphne* then steamed further north out of sight. That afternoon the cutters gave chase to a dhow which was forced to keep out from the shore to avoid them, and consquently sailed towards the ship. She was boarded and found to be a 'legal trader,' with twenty-one slaves on board in a miserable and emaciated condition, lying on the top of her cargo; there were eight men, four women and nine children. Before the boats could return to their former station, another crowded slaver hove in sight, and just as they got up to her, she ran through the breakers, and landed two or three hundred slaves. This was only done by full slavers, the legal traders preferring to pass their few slaves off, if possible, as part of their crew, and of hiding some of them under their cargoes.

On the morning of 1 November, *Daphne* had her first really big success. One of the cutters chased a dhow which had to keep outside her and sailed right into the trap. She lowered her sail, and a few minutes after was brought alongside with one hundred and fifty-six slaves in her, forty-eight men, fifty-three women and fifty-five children. On the bottom of the dhow was a pile of stones as ballast, on top of which, without even a mat, were twenty-three women huddled together—one or two with infants in their arms— who were doubled up as there was no room to sit erect. On a bamboo deck, about three feet above the keel, were forty-eight men, crowded together in the same way, and on another deck above this were fifty-three children. Some of the slaves were in the last stages of starvation and dysentery. On getting the vessel alongside and clearing her out, a woman came up, having an infant about a month or six weeks old in her arms, with one side of its forehead crushed in. On asking how it was done, she told the sailors that just before the boat came alongside the dhow, the child began to cry, and one of the Arabs, fearing the English would hear it, took up a stone and struck it. A few hours after this the poor thing died, and the woman was too weak and ill to be able to point out who had done it from amongst the ten or dozen Arabs on board.

On the same day, 1 November, they took a 'legal trader,' with fifteen slaves on the top of her cargo, who were in very good condition.

Again, on the same day, they took another, with twenty-six slaves in a wretched condition. Some had been brought up from the country south of Quiloa, and fed with a handful of rice and half a coconut-shell of water per day.

The captured dhows contained so little food that Sulivan was obliged to purchase rice from other dhows on the passage back to Zanzibar in order to feed his numerous passengers.

On 4 November, *Daphne* fell in with the *Star* whose appearance was hailed with pleasure by the crew of *Daphne*, for by then it was evident that they had fallen upon a fleet of slavers bound for Muscat, but *Star* was able to carry on the good work begun by *Daphne* whose coal stock was running out. Her upper deck was now crowded with slaves, for it was out of the question keeping them in the dhows, some of which were unseaworthy, and would have sunk if towed.

Mr Churchill, the Consul at Zanzibar, was on his way to Bombay in *Star*, but as Sulivan felt it necessary, under the circumstances, to leave the coast, he ordered *Star*, whose Captain, Commander de Kantzow, was his junior, to remain and intercept the rest of this slave fleet. He then invited the Consul to tranship for the voyage to Bombay. The next morning, after capturing two more slavers in company with *Star*, a total haul of twenty-four slaves was made. The two warships parted company, and *Daphne* steered northwards, with the intention of going to Aden to land the slaves and condemn the prizes. They were unable to get farther than 4°36′ north latitude, where they met the current that always precedes the monsoon, and as the southwest monsoon had now nearly ceased and did not reach so far north at that time of the year, they found themselves with three hundred and twenty-two negroes on board, and only ten tons of coal left, drifting a knot an hour southward. Consequently they altered course for the Seychelles, intending to land the slaves, obtain coal and go to Bombay. But they soon found even this to be impracticable, for by 18 November they had drifted so far down the coast that they had no alternative but to steer for Zanzibar. Three weeks had passed since they left Brava, and they had expended all their coal. On a former occasion they had done the same voyage in only four days.

When *Daphne* sailed into Zanzibar harbour, she had three hundred and twenty-two slaves on board, of whom one hundred and eighteen were men, one hundred and nine women and ninety-five children from a number of different tribes. Sulivan's literal spelling of his interpreter's pronunciation does not assist identification, but these were probably the Wānyika, Segeju, Manga, Chinge, Makua, Yao, Nyasa and Ngindo.

On board ship, the Africans always sat in tribal groups, some of whom appeared to be of greatly superior intellect and more prepossessing appearance than others.

The Galla, in particular, appealed to the sailors as a handsome race; the men powerfully built and the women graceful in form and movement, with their bright, intelligent faces and long curly hair. The Somalis, with whom they were often at war, resembled them in many ways. They were the only people who required animal food on board. All the women were kept on the port side of the quarter-deck, and the ten or twelve Galla women located themselves amidships between the engine-room and after-hatchways, where they received more attention than any of the others, in the shape of an occasional basin of soup, or plate of meat and vegetables brought up from the messes.

The sailors gave their own names to their favourites and the Gallas included Peggy, Susan, Sally, Sophy, Mary, Tom, Jim and others. Peggy was a fine, goodlooking woman with a little boy, Billy, of about twelve months old, who rejected all offers of clothing and toddled about in a state of nudity, and was often to be found in the arms of the Boatswain's mate in the gangway. He was never heard to cry during his six weeks on board.

The Yao people also impressed the crew by their intelligence, but the sailors were not attracted by the women of one of the tribes who were tattooed all over and had large holes in the upper lips, nose, and ears from which rings and ornaments were suspended, and who wore circular pieces of wood in the lobes of their ears.

The most striking man was a Nyika who had escaped from Brava on seeing the ship anchored about two miles off, by swimming against wind and current from the shore, and had actually swum two-thirds of the distance when he was seen from the masthead and a boat sent to pick him up. On his arrival on board he said that he was the slave of a very cruel master, and wanted to escape. On being asked his name, he replied with something that sounded like 'Marlborough.' He was appointed captain of all the other slaves, to keep them in order and superintend the cooking and serving out their provisions—a duty he carried out well—proving a most useful fellow.

For the purpose of cooking, a fireplace was rigged up on raised blocks of wood, having a combing round it covered with sheets of copper, on which was erected a substitute for a stove consisting of raised iron bars for resting the copper vessels taken out of the dhows, under which the fire was placed. Rice and grain formed the chief food, the grain being pounded every morning by some of the men and women. It was then boiled, and served out morning and evening, each tribe having theirs in one large vessel, round which they sat, eating with their fingers.

Each morning, whilst the decks were being washed, all the slaves would be assembled in the gangway, and the steam-hose taken on to the bridge and water pumped over them to their great pleasure. At times a new arrival would get close to the hose, and not knowing its force, he would be knocked down by the stream of water and sent sprawling along the deck, to the great amusement of the others.

Some of the slaves were seriously ill, and a number died, despite the efforts of Dr Mortimer, as they never rallied from the after-effects of exhaustion and starvation on board the dhows. Dysentery carried off others, some suffered from ulcers, and, worst of all, smallpox broke out just before arrival at Zanzibar. It was fortunate that Mr Churchill, the Judge of the Admiralty Court had been able to hear the story of each slave separately whilst on board, facilitating an early departure for the Seychelles, but nevertheless by the time *Daphne* arrived there, fourteen Africans and five sailors were down with smallpox, and thirty-five others of the ship's company were on the sick-list, the largest number during the whole commission, the usual number being five or six.

Sulivan was present during Churchill's interrogations and describes some of them.

A woman of the Galla tribe was the first to come up and when the interpreter handed her a chair, she took her seat in it as if she had been accustomed to one all her life, though perhaps it was the first she had ever seen.

'How did you get on board the dhow?'

'I was stolen with several others from a village.'

'Where is your husband?'

'He was killed in the fight.'

'What is the religion of your tribe?'

'When they wanted rain they went to a priest to get it.'

'Did he pray for it?'

She didn't know.

'When their friends died, what did they do?'

'They took the body to a priest, with a bullock, and he buried it.'

'Who is your god?'

She didn't know.

'Who is the priest's god?'

She couldn't tell.

'When she died, what would become of her?'

She didn't know.

'Was she glad to be free?'

She didn't know she should be free.

'Where are your other children?'

'All stolen from me.'

The next examined was 'Mary,' a very pretty girl of the Galla tribe, about fifteen or sixteen years of age.

'What is your name in your own country?'

'Careesey.'

'What part of the country were you taken from?'

'Teemeto, in Galla country.'

'Are you married?'

'Yes, and my baby died.'

'How were you taken?'

'Stolen with another girl.'

'Who stole you?'

'I was walking with another girl from my hut to my mother's, and two Arabs came out of the bush and took us.'

'How many days travelling were you from your house to the seacoast?'

'One day from Chinacombo at top of river Toolo.'

'Can you see Mount Killamanga from your home?'

'Yes, not far off; but my country is flat.'

'How long was it between your being stolen and captured by the *Daphne*?'

'Ten days.'

'Did you cry or fret much after being stolen?'

'Oh yes, cry much for my father and mother.'

'Were you glad when this ship captured your dhow?'

She did not know she would be free.

'Are many people stolen from your country?'

'Yes, often.'

This girl was one of the first to die of smallpox.

A boy of eight, one of those brought off in the lifeboat from the wreck, said that men stole him and the journey from his country to the coast had taken three moons from the time when the corn was young to when it was cut.

Sulivan was full of praise for his first Lieutenant Acklom, who had used up the last pound of paint in getting the ship ready for an anticipated inspection, and then for six weeks had the mortification of seeing the ship turned into a depot for slaves, who had no special regard for anything on board; and in addition to all this, finding himself the general arbiter of all complaints, for they soon discovered that he was to be looked to for everything.

At the Seychelles, the ship was put in quarantine, and the slaves landed on a quarantine island where a large hut was built for them and a hospital tent erected on the opposite side of the little island for sailors suffering from smallpox.

A few days later, Sulivan visited them and found the interior of the large hut divided off into small huts or rooms, in some of which whole tribes were located, and in other smaller ones, married couples. 'Yes, indeed' he wrote, 'they had taken upon themselves to make the best they could of a world that had treated them so badly, and thus to share their miseries together.'

He took a list of couples, with the names they had acquired or answered to, and sent it to Mr Ward, Commissioner of the island, who promised duly to register the same. The list was headed by Marlborough and Sally, Jim and Peggy, who had been amongst the crew's favourites.

Four months later *Daphne* returned to find about 50 Africans had died, although the sailors had all recovered.

On arriving at Bombay, they heard that *Star* had captured many more slavers, and taken about three hundred liberated Africans to Aden, where doubts were raised in the Indian Court there, as to whether they were domestic. Sulivan wrote in his usual heated and heavily sarcastic vein about these legal queries, as to 'whether it was not wronging the *poor Arabs*, to prevent their taking them to the northern markets, and, further, there appeared to be an inclination to give these *poor Arabs* the benefit of such doubts, and allow them to retain their slaves. I should prefer giving the benefit of any doubt to the slaves, and if either of them are to be abandoned to slavery, why not let the negroes take the Arab back to his country and sell him, as he might in some parts of it possibly, such as the interior of the Galla and Somali country?'

The year 1868 was a good one for the Navy under the energetic direction of Commodore (later Admiral Sir Lionel) Heath, who so disposed the squadron that the slave dealers could never be certain of their movements. Naval Commanders varied in the vigour with which they prosecuted the anti-slave-trade patrols, and as there were never more than six or seven ships available, operating sometimes from the Cape of Good Hope station, and at others from the East Indies (where responsibilities included the west coast of Africa and the Indian and Burma coasts respectively), they were never adequate for the task. Even the following year, the best ever, and the first in which ships operated off the south Arabian coast, fewer than one thousand two hundred slaves were taken. Not only did the dictates of the Commanders-in-Chief and Commodores vary, and for that matter the priorities of the Admiralty, but so did those of most of the individual Captains. Some were more concerned with the bounties that were shared amongst the crew according to an exact scale dependent on rank, and as these were based on tonnage, there was a tendency to exaggerate claims. Others were over-cautious as a result of the occasions when naval officers ran foul of British legalism and apprehended prizes which the Courts interpreted as legal traders, and consequently suffered financial loss. Sulivan was not unique, others were equally vigorous, but he was perhaps the most emotionally committed.

After refitting in Bombay, *Daphne* sailed for the Arabian coast where she chased and boarded some fifty or sixty dhows, all of which had only domestic slaves on board.

After boarding three other dhows, two of which were found to be legal traders, they anchored off Mukulla, in what is now South Yemen, on 26 April. There they found one of the principal markets on the Arabian coast to which dhows went when they were caught by the northeast monsoon and so unable to get further towards Muscat. They would, instead, sell their slaves in Mukulla whence a few would go elsewhere by land. The majority however, stayed until the monsoon changed, when they were sent on to the Persian Gulf.

Sulivan thought that Mukulla was a genuine Arab town, 'the houses are square, built with whitewashed walls, giving the outside some appearance of cleanliness in the distance,' although he was less impressed at close quarters. He went on shore to call on the Sheikh, who appeared to be rather alarmed at the appearance of *Daphne* as he had unpleasant recollections of *Highflyer* two years previously enforcing her demands with a few rounds of shot. Sulivan assured him that his visit was amicable, although he had reason to think there were large numbers of slaves often landed from the dhows, and said that *Daphne* was merely cruising off the coast in order to stop the slave-trade. The Sheikh assured him that if such a trade existed, it was unknown to him, a remark which Sulivan, who disbelieved all Arabs, was not prepared to accept.

On the 29th *Daphne* captured two slavers, one a Zanzibar vessel, having two slaves purchased by the captain at one of the ports on the coast, to be sold again on arrival in the Persian Gulf. The poor creatures cried the whole time they were telling their story, and implored the sailors not to send them back to the dhow. The other was captured by the cutter, whose boarding party was offered a show of resistance, but despite much 'clattering of arms and threatening attitudes,' her crew surrendered without a fight. There were about sixty people crowded on deck of whom about a dozen were Somali passengers. The others were too frightened to say anything except for one woman who had two children with her, although she said that because her husband had recently died, she was being taken by his brother to be sold in repayment of his debts. The two children said that they had been kidnapped by the captain of the dhow about a month before.

On this evidence, the dhow was towed to Aden. Although the woman altered her story in court the dhow was condemned on the strength of the obvious perjury committed by the brother-in-law who claimed that the woman was his wife.

On 11 May, the day *Daphne* left Aden, she captured a dhow with fifty-two slaves on board between the island of Socotra and the Arabian coast.

During the passage to the Seychelles, these liberated slaves appeared to enjoy themselves as they were all in good health and condition, being mostly women and children who were usually well looked after because of their sale value.

At the Seychelles, Sulivan and some of the ship's company paid a visit to Mr and Mrs (Sally) Marlborough and Mr and Mrs (Peggy) Jim, who were living in neatly built huts and said they were very happy and contented. From the Seychelles, they sailed for Zanzibar and began to prepare for a three months cruise towards the south.

This entailed a visit to the retail shop kept by a man known as 'French Charlie,' a half-caste Portuguese in one of the narrowest and dirtiest streets. Inside were great piles of mildewed bags and rusty tins of preserved meat stored against the wall up to the cobweb-covered ceiling. The floor was uneven, and it appeared to be the home of innumerable ants, cockroaches and spiders. An inner room on the right was occupied by several American merchant seamen, and half-caste negro women dressed in Arab costume, in various stages of drunkenness. In the store itself, Sulivan and his officers gave their orders for a sufficient stock of everything required for a long cruise, including goats, fowls, preserved meats, ale, porter, tea, sugar, fruit and vegetables.

Once the supplies were on board, *Daphne* sailed for Dar-es-Salaam, carrying the Consul, Dr Kirk, who was anxious for an interview with the Sultan who was staying in his palace on the mainland. Mrs Kirk accompanied the Consul with their baby, for whom a patent cradle was constructed out of the lid of a box and two chairs. Bishop Tozer was another passenger, as Sulivan had persuaded him that a change of air would do him good after a severe attack of fever.

After an uneventful week, including some fruitless hippo shooting up the river Kingani, *Daphne* was back in Zanzibar with the good Bishop fully restored. The old sailors' adage that a Bishop aboard brings ill-luck was hardly justified, the only incident being a brief grounding on a patch of uncharted coral.

The next day, *Daphne* sailed for Mozambique, where Sulivan's contempt for the Portuguese was as great as his loathing for Arabs. The Africans, on whose behalf he held these feelings, he regarded with paternalistic good humour, referring to their funny 'nigger ways.' The French he viewed with mistrust, and the 'Yankees' with suspicion.

Sulivan described Mozambique as 'an island of one mile-and-a-half in length, situated in a deep inlet of the sea, measuring six miles by five-and-a-half: this inlet receives the waters of three small rivers within the island, and outside lie two small inlets, on one of which St. George's stands, a light house with two men only upon it as light-keepers.'

The population was nearly twenty thousand of whom about eleven thousand were slaves, the remainder—except for the two hundred men of the garrison—being Arabs and Hindu traders. 'To the self-interest of the Banyans,' wrote Sulivan, 'and also to a certain extent to that of the resident Arabs, may be attributed the continued possession of that island by the Portuguese, and were these two races to quit it, the latter could not hold it for a day.'

The other Portuguese settlements were Ibo, an island of four to five miles in length and three across—the most important after Mozambique, and a military station at Quilimane, and one or two places where half-caste Portuguese traded with the Africans and flew the Portuguese flag, only on sufferance by the Arabs, according to Sulivan, who was convinced that Porutugese claims to suzerainty were fantasy. He quoted an instance when an Arab Chief ordered a British Naval officer who had been captured, to be brought to him through country nominally under the Portuguese. When writing of the Portuguese, Sulivan's normal distaste for Arabs was diluted, and he almost implied approval when he wrote ' "Why," say these Arabs, "do you (the English) refuse to acknowledge our power? . . . you see that we have actual possession of the country and always have had it. It is the Portuguese who carry on the slave-trade; we are ready, if recognised, to enter into treaties with the English for its abolition, but while other trades are cut off from us we are compelled to accept that which is forced upon us." '

On the mainland, eight miles from the island of Mozambique, the port of Conducia was the principal Arab town on the coast south of Quiloa. Here there were a few Portuguese villas, but according to Sulivan, these too were only allowed on sufferance, and only Portuguese traders were permitted to enter the harbour, slaves being their chief commodity. Sulivan disagreed with the passage in the recent Report of the Select Committee which stated that: 'The slave-trade in negroes on the East Coast of Africa, is now almost entirely confined to the dominions of Zanzibar,' and insisted that Portuguese abolition was only nominal and that 'the trade is not only as extensive on this part of the coast as ever, but it will be as difficult, if not more so, to stop it here, as in the Zanzibar territory.' Sulivan contended that the committee had not interviewed anyone who had intimate knowledge of the ports in the Portuguese possessions, mainly because there were no resident Britons (apart from one un-unrepentant slave-owner), partly because the Portuguese traded through Arab intermediaries using dhows, and also because the slaves were now called 'free negroes,' and were issued with passports. 'Ask any of the ten thousand negroes, that crowd the streets of Mozambique, where they come from, what they are, and how they got there; and the reply is the same as that of the slaves captured on board the dhows:—Stolen, dragged from their homes and families, sold and bought, sold and bought again, and brought from the markets on the mainland to this place, where they are worse off than they ever were before.'

On 6 September, sailors and marines from *Daphne* boarded a Portuguese schooner bound from Quilimane river, south, to Mozambique harbour, with several slaves including children whose passports showed them to be 'free negroes,' although they spoke no language known to the interpreter, to the Portuguese, or to the Hindu who claimed to be in charge of them; but even Sulivan, who was convinced they had been recently captured in the interior, could not take the risk of detaining the vessel and sending her to the Cape.

Never conceiving it possible, however, that the governor could have decided that these children and the other negroes on board were not slaves, I sent her into Mozambique, to obtain his opinion, with the intention of destroying her if they declared to be slaves. This certainly was a severe test of the honesty of the professions of the Portuguese with respect to the abolition of the slave-trade, and it proved too severe for them; the governor assured me that they were "free negroes," and had passports!

Before going on to defend a hot-headed and debatable action that he took, to the intense anger of the Portuguese in Mozambique and the embarrassment of his superiors, Sulivan referred to 1869 as the year in which

the little power which still remained to the Portuguese was nearly annihilated on the coast . . . a strong force, under one "Bonga," completely defeated the Portuguese troops on the Zambesi, the general and 36 officers being reported killed or missing . . . Angoxa, which had been in the possession of the Portuguese for a few years, revolted, and was taken by some Arab forces . . . In short, the power of the Portuguese, and their only real stronghold, are now, as they always have been, practically confined to the island of Mozambique, their great slave-market.

In support of his claim that slavery had not in fact been abolished in the Portuguese possessions, and perhaps in order to justify his own actions, Sulivan quoted Mr Young (who had searched for Livingstone) as saying of the Portuguese inhabitants that it suited the 'powers-that-be if they are never heard of, least of all in their sole occupation, slavery and its attendant vices . . . The slaver in these dismal mangrove swamps leads a life of incessant terror, lest he should be overpowered by those under him . . . He is alone with his conscience, far from other white men.'

When anchored off Mozambique, where a slave had recently been flogged to death, and where others were in a state of panic, there were attempts by some of them, who hid underneath the wooden pier during the daytime, to reach *Daphne* under cover of night, either by obtaining a canoe or by swimming.

One or two came on board every night while we were anchored there, begging to be allowed to remain. I questioned them as to their condition on shore, when they would point to old and recent lacerations on the back, which they said were produced by the lash; one of them had an iron bar or ring, about an inch in diameter, welded round his leg so tightly, that it was with great difficulty our blacksmith cut it off, and the pain it must have caused the poor fellow when it was soldered on can scarcely be imagined. Those who swam off, there can be no possible doubt, came from the Portuguese town, but to those who came off in canoes, I avoided putting many questions, as it would be required to be proved on·the part of the Portuguese, that they had not come from the Arab town on the mainland, forming the opposite side of the harbour, over which the Portuguese have no authority or power. Sixteen slaves in all came off to the ship to seek the protection of the English flag'

and although a Portuguese official requested their return, Sulivan decided that 'it would have been a disgrace to the flag, and dishonourable on my part to surrender them.'

The official, who turned out to be the Chief of Police, returned to demand the surrender of the Africans, whom he claimed to be 'free negroes.' Sulivan answered that in that case they were free to come on board. The Police official answered that they had no passports and could not stay. Sulivan refused to comply and sailed off with his passengers.

His impulsive and warm-hearted action did not, alas, help the poor Africans who were cooped up on board for the best part of two months as *Daphne* did not put in at any port at which they could have landed as free men. Consequently, when she returned to Mozambique most of them asked to be put on shore again. Two or three swam to a dhow, thinking that the British intended to return them to the Portuguese, but most of the others, given the option by Sulivan, elected to return voluntarily. They were landed, and two returned. Sulivan wrote to the Governor explaining his actions and an accrimonious correspondence ensued.

The most unmitigated falsehoods were published in the Portuguese papers (at Goa, I believe), and also at the Cape of Good Hope, which must have been conveyed there by

the Portuguese corvette lying in the harbour of
Mozambique at the time, on her way home; these falsehoods were only cleared up and proved to be such by a
court of inquiry, on the *Daphne's* return to England in the
following year.

At daybreak on 12 September, *Star* was sighted and
Sulivan learnt of his promotion to Captain. 'The greatest
pleasure afforded by the annoucement was that of the prospect of returning to England, an anticipation that will be
appreciated by those who know what it is to be cruising off
the East Coast of Africa for any length of time.'
Sulivan's orders were to make for Bombay to hand over
command to his successor, but first he set out to extend the
survey they had begun the preceding year of Fernando
Veloso Bay, thirty-five miles north of Mozambique harbour.
Daphne anchored in the snug harbour at the head of the bay
after briefly examining the coast of the inlet and boats' crews
made for the mouth of the river Fernando Veloso where the
entrance was only a few yards across, with twenty fathoms
of water in the whirlpool at the centre, shoaling rapidly on
each side to eight fathoms. Sulivan landed at Sandy Point to
ascertain its longitude, and while so occupied, a number of
Africans made their appearance about fifty yards off in the
bush. Hitherto, as they had pulled along the coast of the bay
and in among the mangroves, they had seen natives paddling
away, as if flying for their lives, in terror at the sailors'
appearance. The British shouted in vain to say that they were
English, not Portuguese; on this occasion, however, a few of
them approached cautiously, and eggs and chickens were
purchased and presents of empty bottles and a little powder
were given. The quicksilver in the artificial horizon used by
Sulivan for his calculations proved a source of unending
delight, and good relations were established. He tried on
several occasions to direct their attention to the white ensign
and to explain to them that 'those who sailed under that flag
never hurt or stole the niggers,' and he believed that many
understood. This incident perhaps more than any other,
encapsulates Sulivan in the context of his time. The
patriotism, the unquestioning belief in moral superiority,

even the delusion that such sentiments spoken in English to uncomprehending Africans, could be understood, were all as much a part of Sulivan as his generosity of spirit and warm heartedness.

On arrival at Zanzibar a few days later, he learnt that Jumah, his interpreter, had died of dysentery, and called upon the widow to confirm that she would receive the balance of pay and prize-money due to her late husband. He went with Abdala, Jumah's servant, who had acted as interpreter since his master's illness, and was at first refused admittance by the male relations until he reassured them that unless he saw Mrs Jumah she could not receive the money. At last, after much vociferous opposition to a Christian visiting a mourning Muslim widow, the objections were overcome, and he was ushered up the stone steps to a room where six or seven women were sitting on a couch. As he entered, they lifted up their hands, wailing and repeating poor Jumah's name. This sorrowful wail was taken up by an invisible person within the curtains drawn around a bed on the left-hand side of the room. This was Mrs Jumah, (the others, he thought, were subsidiary wives), and he was offered a chair close to the curtains. Through the interpreter he promised that everything should be arranged so that she should receive what was due to her late husband through the Consul, and answered many of her questions about poor Jumah's death. She seemed glad to see him, and though unable to speak English appeared to understand it a little. During this conversation she drew the curtains to one side, and then he saw that she was dressed and sitting in the middle of the bed. Sulivan asked her, through Abdala, how long she was going to remain there. She replied that she would stay on the bed for the statutory five months, after which she would remarry on the strength of the prize money.

Sulivan ended the personal part of his memories

Bidding farewell to Zanzibar, to the east coast of Africa, and to all kind friends we had found there: bidding farewell also to Arabs and half-caste Arabs, to Portuguese and half-caste Portuguese, to Banyans and half-caste Banyans; to tortured negroes and torturing half-caste negroes; to markets where human flesh is sold; to fleets of filthy dhows, comparable only to the Black Hole of Calcutta; and to scenes of misery and suffering not surpassed in any age, or in any country,—we left for Bombay where I handed over the command of the *Daphne* to Douglas, and returned in the mail steamer to England.

When *Daphne* sailed for England, her log books for the period of Captain Sulivan's command already filled two enormous, thick, closely written volumes in his precise hand. Not for him the blank or the unfilled columns of some captains: every column has its careful entry: accurate, exact and laconic. Never are details of the course, wind direction, weather, compass bearings omitted, or casually dittoed. Everything is there, ordered, finished and in place: 'weighed and proceeded in chase of dhow . . . boats returned having captured slave and destroyed dhow . . . cutter returned with dhow in tow . . . cleared and burnt dhow . . . hauled alongside, cleared and burnt two dhows . . . cleared the dhows and found the lawful traders.' He 'performed' divine service regularly, and he awarded punishments, he 'read warrant' sentencing men to seven days cells, but no lashes were awarded.

Reading these volumes, with their page after page of neat seamanlike entries, there is no trace of Sulivan the compassionate diarist and humane propagandist for the ending of the slave trade, only Sulivan the professional sailor. His book must have been the safety valve of a generous nature.

It is interesting to read Commodore Heath's annual report to the Admiralty dated March 1869. It showed that sixty-six dhows had been captured and one thousand and ninety-seven slaves liberated, despite the depletion of the squadron caused by the Abyssinian campaign. 'I attribute the results' he wrote 'to the energy and activity of the officers commanding H.M. ships on this station, but something may also be due to the system which had been adopted of pouncing down from Indian ports upon the line of traffic instead of operating, as has hitherto been the practice, from Zanzibar as a centre. Under the new plan the traders remain in perfect ignorance of the intended movements of the cruisers which has not always been the case under the old one.' Commodore Heath did not mince his words, and out of all the annual reports his stand out for their clarity of expression (and, incidentally for the stylish legibility of the handwriting, for everything written by naval officers was done under their own hand, and some is far from legible).

I observe that it is not unusual to close these reports with an expression of hope that the heavy blows which have been dealt at the trade during the past year will go far to check it for the future—I can express no such hope—the trade is far too profitable and will not be affected by a risk so small as that incurred by the proceedings of H.M. ships. It supplies a want which has not been left unsatisfied for many centuries past—a want which, sanctioned by the religion of the country, has grown almost into an instinct. To put down this trade requires far more effort and far more energy than England has yet shown in the matter. Twenty-five years have elapsed since the first treaty with Muscat and all that time we have been content with the capture of a very small percentage of the total exports, a percentage large enough to irritate the legal traders who are harassed and annoyed by the visits of our cruisers but too small to affect materially the illegitimate trade. We must do far more than this to ensure success, we must double or treble our squadron—we must established vice-consultates at the ports of export, above all we must force the government of Zanzibar into active acquiescence with our views, if necessary purchase or take possession of the island.

Commodore Heath attached to his report

some illustrative photographs taken by Commander Sulivan on board H.M.S. Daphne and a water colour drawing by Mr. Hern, Sub-Lieutenant of the ship. The wretched emaciated condition of the slaves shown in the photograph No. 3 is due entirely to the avarice or carelessness of the Arab dealers, but the drowning of men, women and children incidental to running dhows on shore to avoid capture as shown in Mr. Hern's drawing is entirely the result of our proceedings: five full dhows were seen to run on shore during the recent cruise of Daphne and many similar cases have been observed during the year.

'I would most earnestly submit for their Lordships' consideration whether it is right to follow the present unsatisfactory mode of attempting to put down the East African Slave Trade. If I am right in supposing that the only result of these proceedings has been to liberate less than five percent of the slaves exported at the expense of drowning some hundreds a year and of discouraging legitimate commerce it would seem to follow that we should withdraw from the attempt or make it with far greater vigour.'

This was probably the most objective assessment of the Navy's position made by any naval officer.

Today the faded sepia photographs can still be seen attached to Commodore Heath's letter, embedded in a volume of Foreign Office documents in the bowels of the Public Record Office in London. In one, the main deck of Daphne is crowded with slaves, under the cheerful eye of a group of sailors and a marine. Another shows a group of children, and the third is a close-up of a mixed group, listlessly squatting on deck, little more than bags of bones protruding from living skeletons.

Not long after this, Sulivan was to be instrumental in setting a hornet's nest around the ears of the East Indies Squadron. On 16 June 1869 he sent in a report regarding the capture of several dhows, noticeable for what was omitted '. . . after leaving Aden on the 11th May I returned off Maculla and from there steering eastward chased and boarded several dhows, but finding to the eastward of the longitude of Guardefui that the monsoon had evidently set in, I shaped a course for the Seychelles, capturing a dhow on the 15th May with fifty-two slaves on board between Socotra and the mainland. I landed the crew at their request at the east end of Socotra and arrived here (Seychelles) on the 6th instant, where we landed the slaves . . .' but he made no mention of the fate of the dhow which was destroyed.

On 17 September, when Sulivan was home in England, a rather acid letter was addressed from the India Office 'respecting the case of a vessel engaged in lawful commerce, but captured by *Daphne*.' The special attention of their Lordships was invited to a section of a letter received at the India Office from the Government of India suggesting that 'the action of H.M. cruisers might be restricted to cases in which native craft are clearly employed in carrying a number of slaves for the purpose of unlawful sale.'

The Admiralty replied that regulations were being drawn up for the guidance of Commanders with the view of preventing illegal captures, and although this must have seemed appropriate to cultivated civil servants in Whitehall, it only resulted in even greater frustration for naval officers on the spot.

In due course the Admiralty addressed itself to these men in no uncertain terms. 'The attention of the Lords Commissioners of Admiralty having been called to serious irregularities and mistakes committed by officers commanding the ships employed in the suppression of the slave trade on the East Coast of Africa . . . My Lords strongly insist that such destruction of a vessel is only to be resorted to as an extreme measure. Nothing will excuse the officer in not sending in the vessel to a port of adjudication except factors showing satisfactorily that doing so would have involved serious danger to the lives of the prize crew.'

In due course these regulations came out, pages and pages of them in fine legal language. They were met with a plea for a shortened simplified edition for junior officers in charge of ship's boats, who, poor young men, would have to take decisions that would seem so right in a swampy creek or an estuary, and so wrong to legal minds in London.

Fortunately they had a great champion in Commodore Heath, who, writing of another incident in which Dr Kirk had not upheld the action of a Captain (and Captains could suffer considerable personal financial loss if they were not supported—hence the lukewarm attitude of a number of captains towards chasing slavers). 'It is a hardship to the officers commanding on the station that not-with-standing the numerous precedents condemning dhows for having domestic slaves on board etc, they should yet be subject to adverse decisions on this very point.' Commodore Heath then turned to their Lordship's letter regarding the 'unsatisfactory system at present pursued by H.M.'s cruisers in dealing with vessels suspected of being engaged in the slave trade, and suggesting that when there is not a full cargo of slaves on board the vessels with a part or the whole of their crew should be sent to the port of adjudication . . .' 'But it is in most cases practically impossible to take the vessels themselves into port, owing to the strength of wind and currents and I may quote in illustration of the statement the case of the *Daphne* and *Star* in the autumn of last year, the one capturing fifteen and the other twenty-four dhows near Brava and it being as much as the men-of-war could do to reach port themselves, so nearly was their coal expended—to have towed even a single dhow would have been out of the question. It is a mistake to suppose that suspected dhows are always destroyed, their Lordships will observe in many reports that officers have attempted to tow these vessels and been obliged after a few days to destroy them from their weakness . . . The habit of slave dealing either wholesale or retail is so universal amongst the Arabs that I think the reports of some of the commanders under my orders to the effect that almost every large Zanzibar dhow trading to the south carries in the course of its rounds slaves to Madagascar may to a considerable extent be true . . . Their Lordships are aware of my opinion that we are even now doing but little good and that to suceed we must put forth far more strength and energy and that the most efficient step that England could take in this matter would be the purchase of the sovereignty of Zanzibar . . .'

CHAPTER 5

'THE TRADE OF HELL'

Sulivan wrote that one thousand and seventy-one slaves were released in the year 1868, and in the following year one thousand one hundred and eight (according to Heath, the number was one thousand one hundred and seventeen),

> the largest number that had been set free for many years, and so alarmed the Indian authorities for fear I presume that it should rouse the anger of the Imaum of Muscat (sic) and petty chiefs of Arabia and the Persian Gulf, that a Commission was organised and reported that many mistakes and improper seizures were made by officers. As I am not one of those tc whom these charges can refer, seeing that the vessels captured with slaves on board were condemned, I may perhaps be allowed to show that the mistakes, if any, were on the part of those who had given evidence before the Commission.

As usual, he saw the issue so clearly in terms of morality that he had no patience with diplomatic considerations or political expedience, and this time the authorities at home and in India came in for his criticism. He was convinced that British officials in India were being hoodwinked and were unaware of the realities of 'domestic slavery,' that the 'domestic slaves' on board legal traders were usually being transported for sale and that naval officers on the spot were better equipped to differentiate between genuine crew members and slaves passed off as such, than British officials in India to whom Indian merchants turned with their hard-luck stories. 'The stamp of the negro sailor himself, who is so differently treated on board the dhows, and whose intelligence is evidently so superior to any other negroes found there, and the absence of the look of submissive despair in the expression of his countenance, are sufficient to distinguish him, and I know of no mistake of the kind ever having been made.' He supported his argument with the fact that dhows sailing southwards towards the markets rarely had domestic slaves on board, unlike those going northwards and operated with much smaller crews with no dubious 'sailors' amongst them. He reckoned that whilst Zanzibar's domestic requirement was for no more than twenty thousand slaves, at least fifty thousand were imported annually, most of whom were sent northwards.

Is it not preposterous to talk of respect for dhows having so-called "domestic slaves" on board and on their way to the northern markets? I am sure that every officer who has been on the African coast, and has had any experience of the trade there, will agree with me that not one in a thousand of those on board are "domestic slaves," or even return to Zanzibar territory again ... poor creatures, dragged from their homes in the interior, and up from Mozambique to Quiloa and the Zanzibar markets, to find their way to the northern markets in legal as well as illegal traders, by twos, by tens, and by thousands.

From the Great Lakes where Tipu Tib and other Arab dealers of enormous wealth collected the caravans after months of raiding in the interior, the slaves—those who survived—trudged down to the heat of the coast. From there the majority went to the great slave market of Zanzibar, of which Sulivan wrote:

here the first thing that meets the eye is a number of slaves arranged in a semi-circle with their faces towards us in the centre of the square. Most of them are standing up, but some are sitting on the ground. Some of them in fact are utterly incapable of standing upon their feet, miserable, emaciated skeletons on whom disease and perhaps starvation has placed its mark. Inside this circle are half-a-dozen or so Arabs talking together, examining the slaves, discussing their points and estimating their value, just as farmers examine cattle at an English fair or market. In another portion are a number of women forming several semi-circles, their faces are painted and their bodies exposed in proportion to their symmetry with barely a yard of cloth around their hips, with rows of girls from the age of twelve upwards exposed to the examination of throngs of Arabs.

After being purchased, slaves were usually transported by sea to their final destinations. They were taken by dhows of which there were four types, all of which had the common characteristic of single mast and lateen sail which enabled them to sail with the wind astern or abeam, but unable to tack or sail close to the wind. The *Batela* and the *Badeni* were the largest types, some of them up to seventy feet in length; the *Bagala* was a local type built in Zanzibar; and the *Mtepe* was a large barge built of strips of tree bark sewn close together with thongs of hide. All went under the common name of 'dhow' and their modern counterparts vary little in design. They usually had bamboo platforms erected on the deck, leaving a narrow passage in the centre. The slaves were then stowed in bulk; the first lot along the floor of the vessel, two adults side by side, with a boy or girl resting between or on them, until the tier was completed; over them the first platform was laid, supported an inch or two clear of their bodies, when a second tier was stowed, and so on until they reached above the gunwale of the vessel.

Shortly after Sulivan's return to England, the Committee of the Privy Council presented its report which included a general description of the East African slave trade—'The Trade of Hell,' as Livingstone had called it. Before returning to Sulivan's third and final encounter with the trade, it is worth quoting from this description, and from some of the evidence given the following year, 1871, to a Select Committee of the House of Commons:

The persons by whom this traffic is carried on are for the most part Arabs, subjects of the Sultan of Zanzibar . . . These slave dealers start for the interior well armed with articles for the barter of slaves such as beads and cotton cloth. On arrival at the scene of their operations they incite and sometimes help the natives of one tribe to make war upon another. Their assistance almost invariably secures victory for the side which they support and the captives become their property either by right or purchase, the price in the latter case being only a few yards of cotton cloth. In the course of these operations thousands are killed or die subsequently of their wounds or starvation, villages are burned and women and children are carried away as slaves. The complete depopulation of the country between the coast and the present field of the slave dealer's operations attests the fearful character of these raids. Having by these and other means obtained a sufficient number of slaves to allow for the heavy losses on the road, slave dealers start with them for the coast . . . The slaves are marched in gangs, the males with their necks yoked in heavy forked sticks which at night are forced into the ground or lashed together so as to make escape impossible, the women and children are bound with thongs. Any attempts to escape or untie their bonds, any wavering or lagging on the journey has but one punishment, immediate death. The sick are left behind and the route off the slave caravan can be tracked by the dying and the dead. The Arabs only value these poor creatures at the price which they will fetch in the market, and if they are not likely to fetch the cost of their conveyance, they are got rid of. The result is that a great number of the slaves arrive at their destination in a state of the greatest misery and emaciation . . . Kilwa is the main point of departure and ninety-seven-thousand, two-hundred-and-three have been exported in the previous five years. The Sultan levies a tax of two-and-a-half dollars on each in addition to another two dollars for every slave landed in Zanzibar. A slave costs the slave trader nothing to obtain, is worth five dollars at Kilwa, seventeen at Zanzibar and sixty on the Arabian coast.

Mr Churchill, former British Consul in Zanzibar, described to the Select Committee the last accounts of the trade from Zanzibar—

They are very bad; from a private letter I have received, I learn that the slave trade has increased in activity; the policy of Seyd Bargash* (sic) towards the British agency has also altered; he was at first rather frightened at the attitude of the agency towards him; he did not know exactly what the British Government might do, and he was particularly anxious to please; but afterwards, seeing that nothing came of the insolent language he had held immediately after his accession, he changed about again, and became as insolent as ever; as far as the slave trade is concerned, I believe he has not changed his views . . . I think the Arabs do not understand forbearance at all; they put it down to impotency; they think you are not in a position to insist on anything, and they misunderstand the motive; in my opinion, the best plan would have been to have adopted strong measures towards the Sultan, and to have forced him to a certain extent.

Sir Bartle Frere* said in the course of his evidence—

It appears to me that the cardinal evil which you have to deal with is the oscillation of our own opinions in the matter. Up to about the time when Lord Palmerston died, for many years the general opinion of all parties in England had been in favour of a determination to put a stop to the slave trade wherever we could possibly do so without infringing the rights of other nations, and the whole weight of the Government influence had been put on the side of suppressing the slave trade. But of late years it has been manifest that there has been very considerable wavering of our own opinions upon the subject. Many of those who were most active in promoting measures for the suppression of the slave trade in former times have thought, perhaps, that the work was done, and because the work was effectually carried out on the west coast of

*Sayyid Barghash. Consuls as well as naval officers allowed themselves considerable latitude over the spelling of proper and place names.

*Sir Bartle Frere, a former Governor of Bombay and a member of The Council of India, led an abortive mission to Zanzibar in 1873, to persuade the Sultan to abolish the slave trade.

Africa they have rather relaxed their efforts, and one sees in public writings a good deal of a kind of excuse for slavery, which certainly would not have been put forward some years ago . . . and our Government, representing public opinion, appears to me of late years to have been very half-hearted in the matter. The first thing to be done seems to be to make up our minds with regard to what is to be done, and whether we really are in earnest as we were twenty-five or thirty years ago.

Admiral Heath reiterated the arguments he had expressed as Commodore in his final report. He was convinced that the navy could not suppress the trade with its existing limited powers and resources—

For the year ending December 1867, eighteen dhows were captured, and 431 slaves were emancipated; those being the cargoes of the eighteen dhows. During that year, the squadron were all employed in Annesley Bay in the Expedition against Abyssinia, and the efforts against the slave trade were comparatively small. In the year ending December 1868, the total number of vessels captured was 66; the total tonnage of these dhows was 7,233; and the total number of slaves liberated was 1,097. In the year 1869, the total number of dhows captured was 32; the total tonnage of those dhows was 3,431; and the total number of slaves liberated was 1,117. During the second year's cruise my ships were distributed principally along the coast of Arabia, from Ras-el-Hadd as far as Maculla, one being stationed near Socotra, and two down in the Zanzibar neighbourhood. The vessels boarded during the spring season were upwards of 400 dhows; out of those 400 dhows there were but 11 slavers, and in those 11 slavers there were 958 slaves. I am exceedingly puzzled to know how it is that the enormous number of slaves exported get along the coast without being found out. I believe that very few dhows could have passed the squadron during those months; and though, comparing the wants of Zanzibar with the known importations at Zanzibar, there must have been not many short of 20,000 slaves exported, yet it appears that there were not above 1,000 slaves on board these 400 dhows. This rather shows that naval efforts alone will not put down the trade. Referring to the bureaucratic straight-jacket that confined naval officers and to the circular of which Sulivan had been so critical, Admiral Heath said that it

made an unpleasant impression upon all the officers commanding the ships under my orders. Its manner was accusatory as to the past and threatening as to the future; its matter was principally the forbidding the capture of dhows for having domestic slaves aboard . . . I still hold that the only radical cure will be the making Zanzibar a centre from which British civilisation can radiate into that part of Africa.'

Rear Admiral Hillyer agreed with this and described Zanzibar as 'the focus of the slave-trade on the east coast much the same as Lagos was on the west coast . . . As long as the Sultan of Zanzibar derives his main revenue from the slave trade, I think he will encourage it, either openly or under the rose'.

Major-General Rigby* told the committee that if the slave dhows 'happen to sight an English steamer at sea the slavers frequently cut the throats of the whole number of slaves on board and throw them overboard,' and that the presence of the Navy actually increased the sufferings of the slaves, quoting the instance of a dhow captured by *Lyra*.

There were 112 girls on board her, evidently selected to be sold at a high price for the harems of Arabia and Persia. A fatigue party from *Lyra* was sent into the dhow to take out the provisions, but each man as he went into the hold of the dhow fainted away; the doctor then gave orders that the vessel was to be towed out and scuttled, and he said from the frightful stench, and the state the dhow was in, if she had gone to sea, there could be no doubt that in a week the whole of those slaves would have died; that I think is a

---

*Major-General Rigby—a distinguished former Consul at Zanzibar, who had also served in the Gulf and at Aden, and had seen the slave trade at both ends.

very common case. They go to sea so ill provided, that the sufferings of the slaves are very great, and particularly if they have put off their departure to the last, or if the northern winds set in earlier than usual, and they cannot beat up against them; then the sufferings are frightful.

The General thought that the trade could be stopped in five years if there was a coherent policy:

one year you get an active officer on the coast, who enters into the spirit of the thing, and checks the trade a good deal; then he goes away, and another man comes with quite different opinions; or you get a captain of a cruiser who takes the advice of the Consul and pulls with him, and he does a great deal of good; and then perhaps just as he has become acquainted with the secrets of the trade, and begins to know where the slaves are shipped, and where the dhows put in for water, and can distinguish between a legitimate trader and a slave dhow, which it takes a long time to do, he is ordered away, and never goes back again.

It would have been interesting to have heard the sailors' comments on General Rigby's statements, which have a ring of truth about them. But he and they were in agreement that less emphasis on diplomatic methods would have achieved much more—

We should simply say we will not allow this; I think the Arabs quite understand that way of putting it. I often said to the Sultan, you Arabs come down here because you find a very pleasant and fertile country preferable to your deserts, but that does not give you any right to depopulate half Africa, and to go and steal the population and sell them.

On being asked what he thought of the terms of the treaty proposed by the Slave Trade Committee sitting at the Foreign Office in 1869, the General answered—'I do not think any treaty would have the slightest effect; treaties with Arabs are mere waste paper.'

Describing the general state of the trade, he said

The worst part of the slave-trade is that from Lake Nyassa to the south, Kilwa being the port of shipment. The whole of that vast and rich country is becoming depopulated. Banyans who have been for years at Zanzibar have told me that they remember, when they first came to the coast, the whole country was densely populated down to the sea-coast, and you now have to go eighteen days' journey inland before you come upon a village almost. That is fully confirmed by Baron Van der Decken and Rosher, who travelled that route. Baron Van der Decken talks of miles and miles of ruined towns and villages the whole way up towards Lake Nyasa, where there is now no population at all. Every year this slave-trade is extending farther and farther inland. A great number of the slaves are now brought from the western side of Lake Nyasa; the Arabs have got dhows on the lake on purpose to convey their slaves across. I had a proof at Zanzibar of how the slave-trade extends from nation to nation in Africa. I found, in registering all the slaves I emancipated, that amongst the recent arrivals most of them gave the names of their tribe as Mangana. I could not at that time exactly fix the position of their country; however, shortly afterwards I saw a letter of Dr. Livingstone in the paper, saying that he had recently travelled through the Mangana country, where the whole population was engaged in the cultivation and working up of cotton; and he said that he had never seen such a wonderful cotton country in his life, or such a fertile country. I think, a year or two afterwards, he went through the same country, and found it entirely de-populated, all the huts being full of dead bodies. The children had been carried away, and most of the adults slain. That is one of the worst features of the slave-trade in that country. When the slave-traders go into a district, they kill all the men and women, and burn the villages, and carry off the children. The reason they give for taking the children only is that the children are driven more easily, like flocks of sheep, or they are tied with ropes and chains; the men they lose more by desertion on the way.

The Reverend Horace Waller said that there were four types of trade in the area south of Lake Nyasa: in the first the Portuguese collected all the women and children they could in the highlands bordering on the river Shire and transported them thence to Tete, the principal Portuguese port on the Zambesi, from there they were sold to the Kaffir tribes in the interior in return for ivory and gold dust; secondly there was the traffic to Kilimani at the mouth of the Zambezi for the same; thirdly there was the northern trade to Kilwa by Arabs for export to Zanzibar; and finally another route to Mozambique for export to the Comoro Islands, Madagascar and Reunion. By far the largest proportion consists of children because they are not so troublesome to drive and are much easier caught if they attempt to escape. A boy of two years old was worth two yards of calico and a woman might fetch eight. Asked about the conditions of the caravans, Mr Waller continued,

we liberated a gang of about eighty-four slaves one morning and within a few miles of the place where we liberated them we were shown places in the bush where slaves had been killed only that morning. One poor woman had a child on her back which she had recently given birth to and which she was too weak to carry farther and the slave dealer took it by the heels and dashed its brains against a tree. They were all united in a long string, the men being yoked in heavy forked sticks.

Of the Portuguese, he said,

although their Government had abolished the slave-trade in Mozambique, I must say I do not believe it is abolished, or will be abolished without a British squadron to watch it. Up to recently there was no trade whatever in the Mozambique dominions except the slave-trade; the whole business of the Portuguese population was men-stealing and men-selling. At the five chief ports, Ibo, Mozambique, Inhambane and the mouths of the Zambesi, the only trade was in men. Large parties of half-caste Portuguese, led very often by the Portuguese, scoured all the interior, and brought those slaves down to be sold.

He also described

the process of catching the slaves . . . the slave-dealer
goes into the country with so many muskets, and so many
pieces of calico, and he finds out the most powerful chief,
and gives him spirits, and keeps him in a state of semi-
drunkenness the whole time, and tells him he must have
more slaves; he gives him muskets and powder on account, and the man immediately finds out an opportunity
to settle some old outstanding quarrel with some other
chief, and therefore a war breaks out. As soon as war
breaks out, favourable conditions are created for the
carrying on of the slave-trade because famine is sure to
follow in a country where the people are dependent on one
wet season for tilling the ground, for it is only during the
wet season that corn can be sown. Then a chief without
food, and without the means of buying food, will sell off
his people very cheaply indeed. Captures are made in war.
Kidnapping is prevalent all over the country, which leads
again to all sorts of petty disputes and retaliation, and the
more disturbed a country is, the cheaper slaves become; so
cheap do they at last become, that I have known children
of the age of eight to ten years bought for less corn than
would go into one of our hats, and you may easily imagine
where they are bought so cheaply, and where they fetch so
large a price on the coast, it pays the slave-dealer very well
to collect as many as he can, knowing that he must lose a
certain proportion on the way, but also knowing that the
remnant he saves will pay him a very large profit. It is like
sending up for a large block of ice to London in the hot
weather; you know that a certain amount will melt away
before it reaches you in the country as it travels down; but
that which remains will be quite sufficient for your
wants . . . I should say that one-fifth do reach the coast,
perhaps more; but I would also state this, that the Doctor
(Livingstone) believes that for every slave that comes to
the coast perhaps ten lives are lost in the interior.

Many of the Doctor's statements have been discredited,
but he is not a man to exaggerate in any respect; I know

that contrary opinions about the country have been stated, and it has been hinted that he has coloured things rather too highly, but when I was there I had opportunities of seeing the remains of villages in all directions, the population of which had been entirely swept away; I have seen as many as three villages burning in the morning within two hours, and I have seen hundreds of captives carried away from those villages.

The slaves are now brought from great distances in the interior. The belt of country between the Lakes and the east coast is denuded of its inhabitants, and, therefore, they have to be brought from the west side of Lake Nyasa; they are transferred across the lake in Arab dhows; there are settlements of Arabs on both sides of the lake, and the Doctor in his travels has given very accurate accounts of the slave-trade crossing the Lake.

I think as Englishmen, as a people so blessed as we are, and as a people who profess to put down the slave-trade in different parts of the world, our foremost duty is to stop this frightful loss of life, particularly when we consider that there are only a few treaties, which have never been abided by, in our way. The plainer we make things for the Arabs the better; hitherto there has been a vast amount of confusion; they do not know what we mean, and I candidly confess that such transactions as those I spoke of, in which Englishmen have had to do with the slave-trade, give them cause to complain of us, and give rise to complications. I have seen a French ship lying at the island of Johanna, crammed with slaves, with one of our men-at-war within a cable's length of her, and the poor creatures jumping overboard and swimming to us to protect them; and the Arabs would say to us, there is a Frenchman full of slaves, if it was one of our ships you would burn her directly; why do you not go and take her? All these things lead to complications, and the sooner they are simplified by action *pur et simple*, the better.

Having heard the evidence of a great many people the Select Committee reported:

That the Slave-trade in negroes on the East Coast of Africa is now almost entirely confined to a trade between the dominions of Zanzibar on the one hand, and the coast of Arabia and Persia and the island of Madagascar on the other hand, the principal and by far the largest portion of the traffic being in the former direction . . .'

From the evidence laid down before the Committee it appears that the large majority of the slaves are now brought from the western side of Lake Nyasa (a distance of nearly 500 miles from the coast) to Kilwa, which is the principal port of shipment for Zanzibar, and is near the southern limit of the Zanzibar dominions . . .

The whole slave-trade by sea, whether for the supply of the Sultan's African dominions or the markets in Arabia and Persia, is carried on by Arabs from Muscat and other ports on the Arabian coast. They are not subjects of Zanzibar, but chiefly belong to tribes of roving and pre-datory habits.

The sea passage exposes the slave to much suffering; and, in addition to the danger from overcrowding and in-sufficient food and water, the loss of life connected with the attempt to escape Her Majesty's cruisers is very con-siderable, it being the practice to use any means to get rid of the slaves in order to escape condemnation should the dhow be captured . . .

It has also been shown that the slave-trade still exists from the Portuguese territory to the island of Madagascar, and that slaves are still imported into Turkish ports in the Red Sea, General Rigby having recently seen fresh importations even in the civilised port of Suez. It must not, however, be thought that those who are taken captive, great as the numbers are, represent to any degree the total number of the sufferers from this iniquitous traffic. Such are the miseries which attend it, that, according to Dr. Livingstone and others, not one in five, in some cases not one in ten, of the victims of the slave hunters ever reach the coast alive . . .

To control this trade, treaties have been made with the Sultan of Muscat, with the friendly Arab chiefs on the

Arabian coast, and with the Shah of Persia. The treaties with the Sultan of Muscat are acknowledged to be binding upon the Sultan of Zanzibar, who has issued orders accordingly, and they prohibit the export of slaves from Africa as well as their import from Africa into Asia, Arabia, the Red Sea, or Persian Gulf, but permit the transport of slaves to and fro between Kilwa, Zanzibar, and any coast port up to Lamoo, which is the northern limit of the Sultan of Zanzibar's dominions.

The result of the treaties, as far as the Sultan of Zanzibar is concerned, is, that not only are the slave traders enabled to rendezvous in great numbers at Zanzibar, but the dhows, often so laden that the deck is entirely covered with slaves, squatting side by side, and so closely packed that it is impossible for them to move, come up openly from Kilwa, to Zanzibar, and then starting afresh, and provided with proper clearances for Lamoo, are enabled to make the first half of the journey north unmolested by British cruisers.

The object of the British Government in assenting to these treaty provisions was to avoid interference with the status of domestic slavery in the dominions of the Sultan of Zanzibar, as appears by a Despatch from the Right Honourable Earl Russell, dated 14th March, 1864, in which it is stated 'that her Majesty's Government do not claim the right to interfere in the status of domestic slavery in Zanzibar, nor with the *bona fide* transport of slaves from one part of the Sultan's territory to another. So long as this traffic shall not be made a cloak to cover the foreign slave-trade, which his Highness is bound by treaty to prevent, and which Her Majesty's Government are also determined to suppress.'

It appears from the evidence that the transport of slaves between the island and the coast dominions of the Sultan of Zanzibar has afforded a cover for the foreign slave-trade, as the traders procure at Zanzibar or Kilwa the requisite port clearances and passes for Lamoo, and thence run northwards, taking their chance of escaping the British cruisers.

The Committee reported that its members were

strongly of the opinion that all legitimate means should be used to put an end altogether to the East African slave trade. They believe that any attempt to supply slaves for domestic use in Zanzibar will always be a pretext and cloak for a foreign trade, while the loss of life and the injury caused to maintain even the limited supply of slaves required for this purpose, must of necessity be so great as to forbid this country continuing to recognise any such traffic in slaves. It was recommended that a new treaty with the Sultan to establish the entire abolition of the slave trade should be negotiated.

Action followed swifly, in three main directions. First, the Foreign Office instructed Consuls to increase their vigilance. Protests were made to the Imperial Austrian government that African slaves from the Yemen (originally brought there, no doubt, from Zanzibar) had been shipped aboard a Lloyd Triestino steamer at Smyrna, in the dominions of the Turkish Empire, bound for Constantinople. There were, indeed, frequent shipments to Smyrna, most of which were in Egyptian vessels, and Earl Granville wrote to the British Representative in Egypt,

The only effectual method for extinguishing the Egyptian slave trade is to be found in the faithful compliance of the Viceroy and his Government with the firman of January 1857, and I have therefore to instruct you to call His Highness' attention to the frequent shipment of slaves in Egyptian vessels, and to express to him the conviction of Her Majesty's Government that the continuance of this traffic must be attributed either to the negligence or to the still more culpable connivance of Egyptian officials, and you will request that stringent measures may be taken to put a stop to this traffic, and also to punish the parties who may be engaged in it.

Here, as in Zanzibar, Britain had the problem of dealing with an independent ruler, who could be coerced but not commanded.

The second result of the Committee's report was the adoption of the recommendation that the number of Vice-Admiralty Courts be increased, for these were the courts that decided on the legality or otherwise of the trade in which captured dhows had been engaged.

From the New Year onwards, when dhows were captured they were towed either to the port where the court sat, usually Zanzibar, or to the nearest port, or, if they were not seaworthy enough, they were surveyed before being left to sink. Thus the court was able to have the exact evidence at its disposal. This duty of survey was not popular with the junior officers who had to undertake it, as the dhows broke up in a few minutes if wrecked in the surf, making it a hazardous undertaking. Also the normal methods of computing tonnage were difficult to use in these cases as nearly a quarter of the dhow was represented by the huge stern and raised poop.

Kirk himself was the judge of the Vice-Admiralty Court at Zanzibar, and in the following year cases became more frequent, all following an established procedure; the court records contain first a statement of the charge, then the decree of the judge, accompanied by the survey and details of measurement and tonnage. These were all despatched to the Foreign Office, and many of them are still in existence. Behind the dry legal language one catches glimpses of the hardships endured and the type of life led by young officers and sailors.

The third, and most important, consequence was that on 6 June 1873, Kirk was able to write to the Earl Granville: 'I have the honour to report that yesterday afternoon His Highness Seyed Barghash ratified the new treaty for the total abolition of the slave trade in his dominions which had been signed by Seyd Naser bin Saeed the same day on his behalf, and by me on the part of Her Majesty the Queen.'

But more than almost any other Briton connected with the East African slave trade, Sulivan's concern was not solely with the trade itself, the end of which was now, as a result of the treaty, at least in sight, although it was to be nearly a quarter of a century before the chapter was finally closed. George Sulivan was concerned with the after-care of the slaves, their physical and in particular their spiritual welfare, and wrote:

It is seen by the numbers given that the sum total of slaves set free in two years, 1868–69, amounted to 2,179. I am not acquainted with the exact number landed at each place; more than half of them I believe were landed at Seychelles, the remainder—with the exception of a few taken to Bombay, and a few children, selected for his school in Zanzibar by Bishop Tozer in 1868—were carried to Aden. What has become of them? and, Have we in any way improved their condition? are fair questions; there is no institution on this coast similar to that at Sierra Leone on the Western.

He had made enquiries at the Seychelles, and found that rescued slaves were farmed out to the Creoles for five years, after which they were supposed to be able to shift for themselves. Their wages were one pound of rice per day, six pounds of fish per month, and one dollar per month, and they had to find their own clothes. Their material conditions were subsequently improved, but 'in a religious point of view, the liberated Africans, even at Seychelles, are not a whit better off that we are aware of than before.' The resident Anglican clergyman had his hands full attending to the residents, to whom, besides his weekly services, and his work in the schools, he had to preach three times every Sunday, once in English and twice in French. All he could do for the freed slaves was to receive a few of the children in the mission schools. 'The consequence is that at Seychelles they unlearn nothing that was evil in their former lives, while they increase it tenfold by drunkenness and debauchery of every kind.' According to Sulivan, who was far from being unbiased, the Jesuits there who were well entrenched with the Creole population apparently did not cater for the Africans at all.

At Aden, the freed slaves were kept on a small island until they could be sent to Bombay, Mauritius or Seychelles, and there was little or no employment for those who remained. A few had been farmed out to the Parsees, 'a doubtful advantage to them temporally, certainly none religiously, and many we fear have found their way back to slavery again.' Those that went to Mauritius and the Seychelles were employed by the French planters, but there was no after-care, only a few of the children went to school and their parents continued to live in the same state of nudity as in their own countries, a state which Sulivan found offensive. He wrote strongly in favour of increased missionary activity, especially in the field of education, which interested him.

Have we nothing more to offer the liberated negro but his freedom? enhancing as we do in releasing him the misery of ten others of his own race . . . it is England's bounden duty to give at least two years' instruction to every adult slave she liberates, and a fair education to the children.

'If we liberate a thousand negroes a year, which is improbable, we should never have more than two thousand under instruction at a time—which would not be a very costly undertaking when we consider how much money is spent at home in education.

He felt that to place liberated slaves in places such as Mauritius or Zanzibar without widening their horizons, was actively harmful, and strongly opposed Lord Clarendon's scheme to place most of them in Zanzibar under the suzerainty of the Sultan, whom he called 'a cunning Arab and not to be trusted; he might sell dozens of them, and declare that they had been stolen by the northern Arabs.' He wanted a centre for freed slaves to be established on the mainland, so that they could have the chance of returning to their own homes and in due course Freretown was indeed established, on the mainland.

The embankments of the great African reservoir of humanity have been broken down by the slave-dealers; it is of no use trying to catch a fraction of the escaping stream and leave the breach in the walls of the reservoir, we must repair the breaches, not only by abolishing existing treaties and blockading the places of exit, the ports and rivers of embarkation, but we must also build up the walls, and, to some extent, turn back the stream; and this can only be done by establishing a bulwark on the sea coast, to which all liberated Africans should be taken, and to which the wealth of the country would inevitably flow, under the protection and encouragement of the English . . .

When the post-colonial era has been de-mythologized, it may become generally realised that this, in large measure, is in fact what happened, thanks, in part, not only to the objective vision of Kirk and other administrators and missionaries, but also to the more passionate—if at times unbalanced—vigour of Sulivan and a few others like him.

Sulivan's views on 'petty Eastern chiefs' and 'crafty Arabs' were not shared by Kirk, but his proposal that the slave trade should be totally prohibited was the view to which most of the people concerned were now inclining. Even the Sultan, who had been given a fortaste of Britain's power when the Khedive of Egypt had been forced to give up the ports of Kismayu and Brava which he had seized, now began to realize that he could not withstand the pressures much longer, and he deserves greater credit than Sulivan was ever willing to concede for the way in which ultimately he secured the acceptance of his people for this fundamental change in their way of life.

However, Sulivan's vision of a new coastal centre for freed slaves (in due course to be near Mombassa and not Dar-es-Salaam, which he advocated), for a company to open up the interior, for roads, for small upcountry settlements of former slaves and appointed chieftains, for lands to be given to them at a time when Britain exercised no suzerainty anywhere in East Africa, was inspired and not unprophetic.

Some may not agree with his moral judgements and assumptions, others may argue that his view of Africa was clouded by preconceptions, and some may choose not to accept the unpalatable realities of pre-colonial Africa and the colonial achievement, but they must surely agree that despite his over-simplifications, only a man of humanity and foresight could have written:

Africa has to be civilised and Christianised, and eventually must be. When is the work to be commenced? Are we to postpone it for future generations to accomplish? to sit on the cushions, stuffed by our forefathers, and wear them out, leaving no feathers for our descendants? If nations and individuals are judged, so also will generations be, for omission of good as well as commission of evil, and the evil begins where omission of duties ceases. The tides are either ebbing or flowing; they do not cease to flow in all places at the same time, there are always eddies running out before the flow has ceased entirely, but in the end the whole turns. Unless the tide of civilisation continues to advance, unless we as a nation continue to be of some use, as instruments in the hands of the Almighty, as we have been hitherto, in moulding and planning the world into a civilised form, as the Anglo-Saxon race has been forward in doing, we shall surely be put aside like a blunt instrument, and one of a keener edge taken up instead.

CHAPTER 6

LAST ROUND IN AFRICA

The first attempt to persuade the Sultan to prohibit the slave trade ended in failure when he wrote to Sir Bartle Frere 'We cannot sign the new treaty on account of the hardship it involves to us, on account of dread of insurrection, and on account of the ruin which it would cause to the plantations of our subjects . . . you request that we signify to you either our acceptance or our refusal. In one word, *"No."'* Barghash and his senior officials saw that the end of the trade spelt an ultimate end to slavery itself, and feared the effects on an economy based on cloves and an inexhaustible supply of virtually free labour. However, the second attempt reinforced by Kirk's great influence and persuasiveness, the examples of British power elsewhere, of which the Sultan was made aware, and finally the threat of naval blockade, was more successful; and on 5 June 1873, the treaty was ratified, the export of slaves from anywhere in the Sultan's dominions was prohibited, the slave markets ordered to be closed, liberated slaves were to be protected and British Indian citizens were prohibited from possessing or acquiring slaves.

Although this was only the beginning of a story which ended twenty-four years later in 1897, when the status of slavery was abolished in Zanzibar, and although the treaty heralded nearly a quarter of a century of continued evasion of the law by sea and by the development of new land routes, nevertheless, the navy could at last operate without being hampered by the ambiguities of legal and illegal trades, and in 1874 Admiral Cumming was able to write that 'the effect of the late treaty, as far as the sea traffic in slaves is concerned, it most satisfactory.' *Briton, Daphne* and *Vulture* had blockaded the coast to the north of Zanzibar and towards the latter part of the season (i.e. the slave-running season of March, April and May, when the south-west monsoon was blowing), *Philomel* and *Rifleman* had been stationed on the north-west coast of Arabia, but no illegal traders had been encountered.

But the land traffic had so greatly increased as almost to neutralize the results of the Navy's work at sea. To the north, large quantities of slaves (twelve thousand in 1874) went to Somaliland, and in the south thousands still continued to be transported from Mozambique to Madagascar; and there was even a move afoot to use large dhows to convey slaves direct from the north of Madagascar to the Persian Gulf.

In 1874, the year that Freretown was founded near Mombasa as a settlement for freed slaves, the same year in which his mother, Henrietta Sulivan, died, George Sulivan returned to East African waters for the last time to take command of *London*. One of the recommendations of the Committee had been that a permanent guard ship should be established under an officer experienced in the East African slave trade, and there could have been no more appropriate choice for her first commanding officer. *London* was one of the old wooden two-deckers, and had a complement of eight hundred and fifty men. She remained anchored off Zanzibar until 1893 and was to become a familiar sight to many people, not least the freed slaves. She was the base of operations for many expeditions by launches and ships' boats: in 1876 her chief engineer supervised the making of new parts in the workshop of the French mission for *Daisy*, a light cedar-built motor launch which had arrived in Zanzibar without her main shaft and stern tube, left behind on a P & O liner. In due course, the young Scots engineer, Mackay, who prepared the drawings, took her up in sections to Lake Victoria where she served against Arab slavers. Eight years later, Captain Swann of the Merchant Marine took a steel lifeboat, *Morning Star* eight hundred miles to Lake Tanganyika, and as they set forth on their immense journey, their dhow from Zanzibar to the mainland passed *London* and a sailor shouted, 'So long!' 'I hear that sailor's voice even now,' wrote Captain Swann in 1910. 'It was almost like a requiem over no less than three others of my comrades, who, sitting by my side at that moment, had their faces towards their last resting place in Africa.'

One of Sulivan's successors in command of *London*, Captain Brownrigg, who was known as 'Bwana Mzuri' (good) because of the work he did for the freed slaves, was killed in an encounter with a dhow flying the French flag.

1874 and 1875 were, at first, rewarding years for Captain Sulivan. He was the first captain of the first permanent guard ship, for whose estabishment he himself had been an advocate; he was not yet fifty, but very experienced and was at the peak of his career.

In 1875 he surveyed the Rufiji delta to see if any slaves were passing through, as had been suggested, and in his report he wrote that this was not the case, although slave caravans were still passing along mainland routes to the north. He agan stated his views that Britain should purchase the coast line from Dar es Salaam to Mombasa, both of which could then become centres for freed slaves thus making the route between them useless for the slavers. 'The system,' he wrote 'of giving negroes "tickets-of-freedom" and letting them remain in Zanzibar is not less absurd than to write a card "I'm no longer a fox" and hang it round the neck of one and then send him into a kennel amongst hounds.' Rear-Admiral Cummings was more restrained in his views, and in his covering letter forwarding Sulivan's report to the Admiralty, he wrote 'Captain Sulivan appears to hold somewhat exaggerated views.'

1875 was one of the busiest—and strangest—years in Sulivan's life. In January he took command of an expedition to Mombasa, where Abdalla bin Mohammed, the Akida, had declared himself independent of the Sultan and thus independent of any treaty limitations. Although he was a ruler of some enlighenment and there was much to be said in his favour, nevertheless, this action constituted a potential threat to British interests, particularly British-Indian interests, and therefore on 16 January Sulivan, as Force Commander, sailed with Captain Prideaux, the Acting Consul General, on *Nassau* to reinforce *Rifleman* already at

Mombasa. *Nassau*'s crew were augmented by 'two companies of small-arm men from *London* and a field piece;' and *London*'s steam cutter was taken as a 'rocket-boat.' On arrival off Mombasa, they heard that the Akida's troops had destroyed much of the old town and that most of the Indian merchants had fled. After consulting with a local clergyman, Mr Sparshott, Prideaux decided that 'unless a British man-of-war was continually on the spot, or unless the Sultan kept at Mombasa a very much larger number of troops than he could conveniently spare from Zanzibar and his other garrison upon the coast, there would be no possible hope of permanent security to life and property at Mombasa.' Accordingly the Akida was called upon to surrender, and when he refused, the fort was attacked by the force under Sulivan's command. As soon as *London*'s rocket boat, together with those from *Rifleman* and *Nassau* had taken up station, they opened fire, joined by the guns of the two ships. A number of the forty-nine guns on Fort Jesus returned the fire as the naval force slowly steamed towards the fort. *Nassau* and *Rifleman* anchored where the channel narrowed to less than four hundred yards from the shore, almost underneath the great looming walls of this seemingly impregnable fort which had withstood so many sieges and seen so many bloody conflicts since it was built by the Portuguese in 1594. Although the fire of roundshot and musketry was wildly inaccurate, it was uncomfortable, especially for the sailors in the three open boats who had to pass close under the batteries—fortunately too close for depressing the guns, but none the less unpleasant—in order to take up their final position. After a time, firing from the fort ceased and *Nassau* and *Rifleman* steamed to within two hundred yards, keeping up a heavy fire all the time until it was seen that the Akida's colours were being hauled down.

The next day Prideaux and Sulivan with a force of small-arms men from the two ships marched into the fort, hoisted the Sultan's flag under a general salute and the keys of the fortress were delivered to the Governor. That afternoon they returned to Zanzibar with the Akida and three of his chiefs on board. In his report, Prideaux commended Sulivan's command of operations, and his contention that had the rebellion succeeded, the Akida's example would have been followed by other subordinate rulers 'and a new and unfavourable phase introduced into our slave trade policy' was subsequently supported by the Foreign Office whence a communication was received in March stating 'Lord Derby considers it very probable that if an example had not been made of this rebel chief other petty chiefs on the coast would have attempted to set the Sultan's authority at defiance with the view to carrying on a traffic in slaves on their own account . . . when we should have had several independent chiefs to deal with in the place of one long established authority.'

In May, the request of Commodore Heath of years before, supported by Sulivan, that young officers should receive a simplified form of guidance on their legal obligations regarding the slave trade, at last bore fruit, and a small booklet was issued for these young men who had to shoulder an enormous burden of responsibility, and take immediate decisions in circumstances very different from those in which the law officers of the Crown read and criticized them.

Meanwhile, the boat's crews of *London* were kept busy. Sulivan gives some accounts of actions in his book, but it is interesting also to see how he reported them officially, especially those where only circumstantial evidence existed. Here are two examples:-

No. 1, 13 tons. This dhow was observed by one of the launches on the night of the 23rd of January last entering the harbour of Kobane where she (the launch) was lying at anchor. Immediately however on the launch being perceived by the people on board the dhow, they put her helm up and ran her ashore on the island of Makongui—twenty minutes nearly elapsed before the Sub-Lieutenant in command of the launch got alongside the dhow when he found the Nakoda, three crew and two male persons being of a most contradictory nature and information having been obtained from the shore clearly indicating that the dhow had been engaged in the transportation of slaves as recently as that day, she was brought into court on the 1st

Febry. and on the evidence of a native of Kobane who had seen the slaves landed from her together with other suspicious circumstances connected with her, was condemned.

No.3. *Claura* 42 tons. This dhow was intercepted by the steam pinnace on the 14th February about two miles from Kobane on the island of Pemba, for which port she was making—She had 48 male and female slaves on board which had been shipped at Pangani on the mainland and were intended for the plantations on Pemba—Taken into Court and condemned on 26th February.

Sometimes the Court upheld the assumptions of naval officers such as that of Lieutenant Holt, who boarded a dhow that had run ashore on sighting the launch; although the only evidence had consisted of large casks of water. On other occasions judgement was given in favour of the dhow's owners as when a Sub-Lieutenant had a dhow destroyed which was unsafe to make the passage to Zanzibar as a result of damage sustained when run ashore. The three female slaves on board were found to be domestic slaves, contrary to the statements made to the young officer.

There were a good many others towards the close of the year. In one dhow ten sets of slave irons were found under the cargo in the hold and about ten fathoms of chain, of the kind for connecting the slaves in gangs, which were hidden in a bag of rice found in a locker of which the Nakoda had the key.

In another case, a vessel was left in the charge of a prize crew, but 'owing to the filthy state of the dhow and her being over-run by rats the men could not live on board and they were therefore removed by Sub-Lieutenant Grassie. The same night that this was done the dhow was plundered of her cargo and set on fire, it is supposed by some of her own crew.'

During this period immediately following the Treaty, the Navy was busier than ever, and similar actions to those undertaken by *London*'s boats were being performed by boats' crews of other vessels elsewhere on the coast, as well as pursuit by their mother ships of dhows in the open sea. In the ten years between 1875 and 1885, two hundred and fifty sailors died of wounds or disease sustained on this arduous service.

Unfortunately Sulivan's command of *London* was terminated rather suddenly by a somewhat bizarre incident, but before this occurred, he wrote his final report, as Senior Naval Officer, on 17 November 1875, a statement that was like a trumpet blast to shake the complacency of those who thought that the signing of the treaty meant the immediate end of the slave trade.

He wrote that slaves were being taken overland in large numbers in those coastal areas frequented by cruisers, although the sea route continued to be used in the waters where naval ships were seldom seen. Although only a few canoes were taking slaves from the mainland. to Zanzibar, dhows were still sailing from the mainland areas and islands in the north, and Sulivan regretted that no ships had been cruising off that part of the coast for the past two years during the months of October and November at the close of the southwest monsoon and the northern slave trade season. He returned to his favourite theme that no treaties and no efforts, however great, would lessen the traffic to any extent until more was done for liberated Africans. 'The mere casting them adrift in the Sultan of Zanzibar's dominions, with a percentage of them domiciled at the mission farms (by this time full to overflowing) instead of placing them at some British settlement on the mainland which might be purchased or taken, appears but to be trifling with the negro at an enormous cost to the nation . . .' He even went so far as to doubt whether slaves were any better off for falling into British hands, and reckoned that they themselves would probably not think so, although it would be difficult to identify any of those who had been liberated in the past twenty-five years. 'Religion and Education, Trade and Agriculture must go hand in hand in their advance towards the interior of Africa. In this advance they will be met and joined by the rapidly extending Cape Colonists and the Slave Trade abolished not by the capture of slaves or slavers, nor the acquirement of new slave treaties but by the intermingling of Races and their dependence on each other.'

This was Sulivan's swan song in East Africa, ended by an extraordinary occurence which does not seem to have unduly affected his career, and one that could only have happened to a man of his nature.

A long-standing quarrel with the chaplain aboard *London* erupted into open warfare over the latter's wearing of vestments at services. The upshot was that Sulivan was relieved of his command of the *London* and replaced— ironically—by his cousin, Captain B. M. Sulivan, whose subsequent reports continued the pungent family tradition.

Sulivan himself addressed memorials to the Queen, and wrote at length. Acres of newsprint were expended on it, and it was debated in Parliament where opinions on a dispute that exasperated his seniors became a *cause celèbre*. The actual 'crime' itself is one of such an apparently esoteric nature that it would seem to be one thousand rather than one hundred years removed from modern secular society.

For fifteen months a dispute had simmered between Sulivan and the *London*'s chaplain, Mr Penny, a High Churchman, to whose wearing of a stole with gold crosses worked in yellow floss silk, and to whose services, which included 'chanting' Sulivan strongly objected. Penny insisted, with some justice, that stoles were sanctioned by Bishops, that their decoration with crosses was permitted, that his services were in accordance with the ritual of the Church of England and that no-one else had objected to him. Sulivan reminded Penny that the whole ship's company came under his orders and flagrant disobedience was prejudicial to good discipline. Penny replied to the effect that he owed nothing to a non-conformist captain to whose religious views only a small proportion of the crew subscribed. Sulivan refused to take Holy Communion from Penny's hands because of the 'hoard of unrealistic novelties' introduced into the Service, and walked out of a sermon in which he was criticized, and ordered the services to be shortened by limiting the 'chanting.' In reply, Penny refused to speak to Sulivan. Although an Admiralty letter acknowledged that 'my Lords are of opinion that Mr. Penny's conduct has in several instances

been highly disrespectful towards his Captain,' Admiral
Cumming, to whom the matter was thoroughly irksome,
refused to hold a Court of Inquiry and asked Penny not to
wear the stole if it gave offence. Penny then wrote to the
Admiralty refusing to do this, and as the Admiralty were dis-
inclined to take action, this seemed to Sulivan to be a public
victory for the Chaplain. Certainly Penny became more
aggressive and even the Admiral now reported that he 'had
acted in a spirit apart from that which should be shown by
any officer and especially by a clergyman' and that he would
have to take serious action if this contnued. In the stifling
heat of Zanzibar, tempers became frayed and good sense
receded. Sulivan accused Penny of 'an indecorous way with
negresses in the public streets' and of being drunk on duty
one day, and Penny defended his wine expenditure for that
day as being solely: '1 bottle of light claret (1/6d.) 1 glass of
sherry (3d.) and 2 glasses of brandy at 1d.'

In July 1975, Admiral Macdonald took over command of
the station, and on instructions from home ordered a Court
of Inquiry whose report was sent to the Admiralty who
commented on the findings: 'After a careful perusal of the
whole correspondence commencing as far back as September
1874 my Lords have been compelled with regret to come to
the conclusion that Captain Sulivan has not acted towards
Mr. Penny with that consideration and judgment which is
expected from the Captain of one of Her Majesty's ships.
My Lords are further of opinion that Mr. Penny's conduct
has in several instances been highly disrespectful towards his
Captain; and as they entirely agree in the opinion of the
Court that so long as these two officers remain together no
harmony can be expected, they have decided to remove them
both from the ship, and they are to be so informed.'

Unfortunately Mr Penny was not removed until later, and
had the satisfaction of seeing his Captain over the side.
Sulivan returned to England where he engaged in furious
correspondence and pestered the Admiralty with his
demand for a Court Martial so that all the facts could be
made public and in due course this was debated in
Parliament. The Admiralty line put forward by Mr Hunt was

that Sulivan had incurred no punishment, having only been relieved of his command, although he had acted injudiciously. Mr Hunt quoted Commodore Hewitt as being satisfied that Sulivan's charges against the Chaplain were imaginary, and said that although the Commander-in-Chief was not satisfied with his conduct he was willing to have treated it as an exceptional incident in his career. He knew how fiercely the *odium theologicum* burnt in some breasts, and he was willing to make allowance for it and for the excitement produced by the temperature of Zanzibar . . . The motion was debated that Sulivan should not have been removed from his command without having been given an opportunity, if he desired it, of explaining or defending his conduct before a competent court; and the proposer, Mr Evelyn Ashley, concluded a forceful speech by remarking that 'it seemed to be the opinion of the Admiralty that an officer in command of one of Her Majesty's ships should combine the indifference of a Galileo in religious matters with the tact of a Talleyrand in the affairs of the world.'

Although the weight of opinion in the debate seemed to be largely in Sulivan's favour, the motion was lost by a small margin, although this did not stop him from continuing to petition all and sundry, including the Queen.

The press in England dealt with the affair according to their lights: *Punch* made ponderous fun in prose and verse. The *Newcastle Daily Chronicle* wrote of 'another Admiralty scandal,' *The Times* came down heavily in Sulivan's favour. The *Daily Telegraph* was equivocal, the *Graphic* referred distastefully to the prospect of Mr Penny's 'martyrdom,' the *Scotsman* and the *Noncomformist* as might be expected, had little good to say of Mr Penny. The *Church Times* was fearful of the dangers of 'ritualism afloat' and the *Christian World* expressed its dislike of high church practices. Sulivan seemed to have come to no immediate harm although several correspondents hinted at a 'black influence' at the Admiralty; and Sulivan himself later complained of lack of due recognition because of 'The Penny' case.

This was not the only publicity he had to endure for in

1876 he also engaged in inconclusive litigation with the *Western Morning News* for publishing a letter from a correspondent in Zanzibar complaining that *London* was being misused. 'Besides being fitted out at a very great cost for the purposes of being a store, receiving factory, hospital and prison ship, she was also supplied with 19 boats for cruising purposes, among them 5 excellent launches, 2 whale cutters of 35ft. length, a steam cutter and a pinnace and one of Admiral Hall's patent cork cutters; yet,' complained the correspondent, 'only 72 slaves had been captured after a 10 month blockade whilst 7000 had been landed at Pemba and Zanzibar.' Writing that it was no fault of the officers and men he blamed only Sulivan for wasting time on a survey of Tanga harbour which 'no one has ever used and nobody ever intends to use;' that even so the survey was done badly and that a theodolite had not been used, and went on to criticize the use of three of the boats in a sailing match for a brass chanticleer. In a later edition, the correspondent wrote that *London*'s boats 'lay idle at their moorings . . . To an outsider it seems strange that after a few captures the boats should be left at the moorings off *London* for a considerable time, which does not seem the way of doing things.' George Sulivan must have echoed his brother Bartholomew's view of journalists and newspapers. The writer showed no understanding of the sea service, that boats need maintenance, men need rest, and that a ship's crew has multifarious duties; nor did he appear to appreciate the peculiar difficulties under which the Navy had to operate in the waters of an independent ruler.

In 1876, he gave evidence to the Commission inquiring into the reception of fugitive slaves. In answer to questioning he said that he thought that there was as much slavery, with greater suffering as ever there had been, although fewer slaves were carried by sea. The islands still needed a large number for the clove harvests, and the pretext of domestic slavery facilitated collusion: 'it is as impossible to separate the condition of a domestic slave from that of a new slave as it would be to separate milk from water when mixed.' He repeated his often expressed view that the slaves became worse off after liberation if sent to the Seychelles, and that another colony should be established. He said that as many women were taken off dhows by HM ships as men and that most were destined for the Persian Gulf and from thence to Arabia and Persia.

He remained convinced that the only answer was a settlement on the mainland in which the children could be educated. (It should be remembered that at this time Britain did not govern or control any part of East Africa. The Imperial East Africa Company was not formed until 1888, Zanzibar became a Protectorate in 1890 and the status of slavery not abolished until 1897. In 1876 Sulivan's ideas were by no means generally acceptable politically). He described the incident in *Daphne* when he had clashed with the Portuguese, refusing to give up the slaves that had sought refuge, and other cases of fugitive slaves coming on board. Referring to the continuance of the trade he said: 'we had information last year of between 2000 and 3000 slaves being marched up to Kilwa, up the coast by land . . .' Although the sea traffic from Kilwa to Zanzibar had lessened, it had increased from small and unknown ports . . . 'A dozen at a time will be sent from the north end of Zanzibar to the south end of Pemba, thence to the north of Pemba; then they watch their opportunity for they learn where our boats are, and if they think that they are out of the way, they send the slaves further north again in dhows.'

He suggested the setting up of an *entrepôt* north of Tanga (hence his surveying activities) which would help to curb the trade carried on by Somalis. He told the Commission that the Sultan's powers hardly extended inland where the effects of the treaty were negligible. Referring to domestic slavery, on which he was pressed by the Commission, he had to admit that if a known domestic slave took refuge on board he had been forced to return him to the owner, such being the law of the land. He did not add that of all naval officers, he was the least likely to do this. Finally he gave his views on laws and lawyers, which were less than complimentary.

Their Lordships at the Admiralty were wise enough not to allow him too much time in which to indulge in passionate advocacy and make new enemies, for he was, in the same year, appointed to command the corvette *Sirius* (1,268 tons) in the blockade of Dahomey and for the first time found himself confronted with the slave trade on the other side of Africa.

The West African slave trade differed from the East Coast trade in that it was more cosmopolitan and for four centuries had been mainly conducted by Europeans, the British interest beginning with the voyage of John Hawkins in 1562. Something like five million Africans were transported between the end of the fifteenth and eighteenth centuries and British ships, sailors and merchants, in Bristol, Liverpool and the West Indies were amongst the prime movers in this trade. British evangelical reformers, politicians, diplomats and sailors were to be in the late eighteenth and nineteenth centuries the prime movers in its abolition and suppression.

The slaves were obtained by barter with native chiefs who waxed fat on hunting into the interior, and thus the trade kept the whole coast and hinterland in a permanent state of war. Thousands of people were rounded up and driven through the forests to the coast, where they were imprisoned in slave stockades, called barracoons, described by Commander Forbes, as 'sheds made of heavy piles, driven deep into the earth, and lashed together with bamboos, thatched with palm leaves. In the barracoon, if it is a large one, there is a centre row of piles; along each line of piles is a chain and at intervals of about two feet is a large neck-link, in one of which each slave is padlocked. Should this method be deemed insufficient, two, or sometimes in cases of great strength, three, are shackled together, the strong man being placed between two others and heavily ironed, after being beaten half to death beforehand to ensure his being quiet . . .'

The barracoons were usually on estuaries, and embarkation took place when lookouts reported no cruiser in sight. One such officer described the slaves' plight on board: 'The form of stowage is, that the poor wretch shall be seated on the hams and the head thrust between the knees, and so close that when one moves the mass must. In this state, nature's offices are performed, and frequently, from the maddened passions of uncivilised men, a fight ensues . . .' Another naval officer wrote of a captured Brazilian brig 'The extent of human misery encountered, as evinced by these unfortunate beings, is almost impossible for me to describe. They were all confined in a most crowded state below, and many in irons, which later were released as soon as they could be got at. The putrid atmosphere emitting from the slave deck was horrible in the extreme and so inhuman are these fellow creatures that several of those confined at the farther end of the slave room were obliged to be dragged on deck in an almost lifeless state and wasted away to mere shadows, never having breathed the fresh air since their embarkation. Many females had infants at their breasts, and all very crowded together in a solid mass of filth and compost several suffering from dysentery, and although but a fortnight on board, sixty-seven of them had died from the complaint.'

The voyage was divided into three 'passages:' the outward one, with a cargo of textiles, hardware, alcohol and firearms, which were traded on the coast with chiefs and contractors for slaves who were shipped to America and the West Indies—the middle passage—where they were exchanged for a cargo of sugar, tobacco and rum on the home passage: all three voyages were sailed with prevailing winds.

The slave coast itself extended from Cape Verde in the north to Angola in the south, a distance of three thousand miles and by the time of the abolition of slavery in Britain in 1807 and of the British slave trade in 1833, it was so well established that the navy's task for the rest of the century in trying to suppress it was herculean as the profits were enormous and the risks worth taking. Brazil was a leading importer; so was the USA, and it was not until after the Civil War that America began to look seriously at her nationals engaged in the trade. As France was deeply suspicious of Britian's motives, international action was very difficult. As in East Africa, naval officers had their hands tied to some extent and Captains had to acquaint themselves with the details contained in a fat volume of 'instructions for the guidance of HM Naval Officers employed in the suppression of the Slave Trade,' and an officer could be sued for illegal seizure, or could create an international incident. No wonder that naval officers varied in their enthusiasm for this work, especially when the right of search by British naval vessels was not conceded by other powers. As late as 1882 no British ship could search a French one suspected of slaving and the Americans were equally touchy; and when British and American officers on the spot concluded their own mutual agreements they were disavowed by the governments.

Sulivan had arrived at a situation that was familiar in some respects but was deeper rooted and far more complex than he had known on the East Coast. No wonder he was impatient at the slowness of proceedings.

The Kingdom of Dahomey was the largest slave holding state in West Africa and had been the most reluctant to sign a suppression treaty. Its capital was Abomey, The City of Blood, and Whydal was the great slaving port. Thirteen years before the King—Gelele—had refused to enter into a treaty with Commander Wilmot, who said 'England had been doing her utmost to stop the slave trade in this country. Much money has been spent and many lives sacrificed to obtain this desirable end, but hitherto without success. I have come to as you to put an end to this traffic and to enter into some treaty with me.' The King's answer was 'Nothing will recompense me for the slave trade;' and the following year, even Sir Richard Burton was unable to make the King change his mind, although he was able to tell him that since Lincoln had become President there would be no more American traders.

After this, there was considerable local pressure for Britain to annex Dahomey for a number of reasons: some naval officers and others wanted more pressure exerted to end the slave trade; and there were also officials and business interests who wanted an increase in revenue; and in 1876 a pretext for intervention was provided by the fining of a mulatto trader, José Santos, by the Yavogar, or Viceroy of Whydah. A British Agent, a Mr Turnbull, who protested, was stripped of his trousers and confined for two hours. In evidence he said: 'I was forcibly stripped by an armed assembly and afterwards incarcerated in a filthy cell for some hours besides being very roughly used and for simply protesting against the seizure of the firm's goods. The matter will bear the fullest investigation and all the Europeans are of the opinion that I behaved most creditably.' Then, in a bellicose vein, he went on to demand that a gun boat should 'come to this port at once to inquire into these affairs. I do not know to what further lengths these people may go . . .' After naval officers had tried to obtain redress from the Viceroy—who replied in evasive terms—Commodore Sir William Hewitt ordered Gelele to pay a fine of 500 puncheons of oil (80,000 gallons, worth about £6,000), and threatened to blockade Dahomey if full payment were not received by June 1st. It is possible that Hewitt, who had referred to Gelele's 'diabolical practices' deliberately put the figure so high, in order to have a pretext for attacking Dahomey.

At home however, Lord Derby, who had no use for a military expedition in Africa, regretted Hewitt's course of action but was unable to disavow it without loss of British prestige. Gelele refused to accept and was shrewd enough to indicate that 'the palaver' came not from the Queen but from Hewitt who should 'stop all war palavers and be a merchant, turning his vessels into sailing ships, and loading them with rum, cloth and other merchandise . . .' This answer made it impossible for the Government to climb down, and although Hewitt was rebuked for not referring the matter back to England, he was authorized to enforce the blockade. However, in addition to instructions to 'proclaim that portion of the sea coast of the Kingdom of Dahomey comprised between the longitude of 10°37′ W and the longitude of 20°35′ E to be in a state of blockade,' Commander Powlett, the Senior Naval Officer, was also sent by a cautious government four boxes of Phillimore's *International Law* 'for his perusal.' As always, the sailors wanted action to stop the slave trade, which they saw at close quarters, whilst the more urbane view was taken at home by others like the Under-Secretary at the Foreign Office who wrote that Hewitt's demands amounted to a 'tyrannical use of the opportunity for punishing the Dahomans for being savages . . . a gun boat policy to back a trade quarrel.'

The French, who were deeply involved in trade in Dahomey now took fright, although they had originally supported Turnbull. A blockade, or worse still, British occupation, would injure their trade, and Règis, a leading merchant, told the Colonial Department in Paris that he would help pay the fine himself and advocated French suzerainty over the Dahomey coast line, but the French home government was no more interested at the time in African adventures than were the British. However, they did raise legal objections regarding the extent of the Dahomey coast line, claiming part as French territory and that other areas were independent principalities. Hewitt was not prepared to concede the French rights and indeed the French themselves appeared to accept the inevitability of British military intervention. However, neither the British nor the French metropolitan governments wanted this, for their preoccupations were elsewhere, principally the Middle East. Sir Robert Herbert, Permanent Under-Secretary for the Colonies, even suggested remitting the fine in return for Gelele relinquishing fiscal control of the Dahomey coast, in order to reverse 'the unjust and impolitic note of foolish officers.' Perhaps it was fortunate for Britain that there were objective civil servants and disinterested politicians, but perhaps it was equally fortunate for the oppressed that there were sailors who saw issues of good and evil without diplomatic blurring of the edges, and were prepared, like Sulivan, to allow their hearts to rule their minds. Lord Derby feared that negotiation would lead to war and wrote 'annexation of more West African coast will be very unpopular.' To the naval officer, annexation meant the virtues of British rule and the end of the slave trade; to the politician it meant expeditions for little apparent return: and to liberal sentiment it represented imperialist aggression. Various diplomatic face-savers were attempted and in January 1876 a French agent in Whydah suggested to the Viceroy that Gelele might write to express his regret at Turnbull's treatment, and at the same time request a reduction of the fine, in which case the French would provide the oil. Gelele, however, regarded his independence and prestige as more important than commercial profit, and he was indeed less affected by the British blockade than the French merchants.

Ultimately a similar compromise was agreed to and a letter arrived in London, written by a French agent, with a cross appended, presumably by Gelele, which was accepted with some alacrity and the fine reduced. On 12 May the Viceroy signed a treaty reaffirming the old and broken promises to prohibit the export of slaves and to protect British traders. Ironically enough, the two hundred small puncheons of oil, most of it provided by the French, were all lost when the ship taking them to England was wrecked and the second instalment never arrived and was quietly forgotten.

Before this, Sulivan, commanding *Sirius*, a screw corvette, had taken command of the blockade in its later stages and allowed his views to be known in no uncertain terms—that such a compromise would be regarded as a success for the French merchants. The blockade lasted for less than a year, and during that time British ships effectively prevented any seaborne trade with Dahomey. Sulivan has left no account of these duties, but they were arduous and exacting, having to contend with the usual rigours of climate and inadequate resources.

When it was all over he received the approval and approbation of the Lords of the Admiralty and the concurrence of Lord Derby in their Lordships' opinion that 'Captain Sulivan has throughout conducted this business with zeal, ability and discretion.'

It is interesting therefore to go a little further into what really was Sulivan's part in the whole affair. He took over from Commander Powlett towards the end of 1876 and his first report of any length was to the Secretary of the Admiralty to say that he had called on the French Admiral Ribourton, who thought the fine was too heavy and that the king might pay if it were mitigated, to which Sulivan had replied that the king would misconstrue such an action as weakness—the effects of which might be to increase and prolong difficulties that might arise, 'and would be certain to arise with such savage races, if they fancied they had gained their point in the smallest degree.'

George Sulivan was in many ways a simple man, and his character emerges strongest towards the end of his life: impulsive, emotional devout, upright, with an ingenuous sense of humour, and an uncomplicated attitude towards what he conceived to be good and bad. He was as warm-hearted towards the sailors under his command as to freed slaves and his indignation was easily aroused at brutality and what he thought to be savagery. To him there were no shades, no conflicts of loyalty, no differing codes, no complexities, and no pretexts. Other naval officers took a more balanced view. Writing of the East African trade, Admiral Cumming, who had already indicated that Sulivan allowed his heart to over-rule his head, wrote of Sultan Barghash in 1874, 'his refusal at first to sign the treaty was the will of his chiefs; had he signed it independent of them he would not have lived another day.' Nearly a decade earlier, Captain Bowden of *Wasp* had written: 'The Sultan is perhaps sincere in his wish to prevent the export of slaves to Asia, but he receives no support from any of his subjects and dares do no more than he has . . . The whole seaboard population is Mahommedan; they, thinking slavery a Divine right, cannot understand our views and are consequently partly hostile to us and ask why we, a great nation, steal their slaves when we can buy them so cheaply.' So on the West Coast Sulivan was to meet both British and French naval officers who saw that the actions of the King of Dahomey were inevitably conditioned by the custom and tradition of his kingdom. However, if the world were composed entirely of balanced thinkers, few of the great humanitarian movements, lost causes or great crusades would ever have taken place. We should not judge Sulivan too harshly. To him, if a Sultan or a native king appeared to have radically alien standards and condoned slavery, then he must be a savage and Africa would be better without such rule and under the beneficent protection of a Christian power; and, for that matter,

Christian Portuguese, French, Americans and any others who condoned or took part in the slave trade and whose motives were devious were equally distasteful to him. Nevertheless, he—and others like him—should not be dismissed as caricatures or self-righteous hypocrites, and to understand them it is necessary to realize the depths of their convictions in the rightness of the Christian faith as exemplified in fair dealings towards all men. Perhaps Sulivan was more impulsive than most—but he was also more humane than most, and more sensitive to suffering.

On 17 March 1877 he wrote to his cousin, Commodore Sulivan, then commanding the West African Station to say that the blockade was having little or no effect on the King or people of Dahomey, except possibly in the immediate vicinity of Whydah, that there was an enormous increase of canoe traffic which was impossible to prevent and that there was constant communication with Lagos by way of the lagoons; in fact he himself had received a letter from England that had probably arrived by this source. He advocated a 'well organised surprise attack on Whydah which would meet with little resistance, and would be welcomed by the people.' He wrote that unless the blockade was followed by action, it would be construed as weakness: 'my conviction is that the foreigners (more especially the French) are playing a diplomatic game against us in which we have the disadvantage of holding a dummy hand . . . it would appear their wish to persuade the King of Dahomey that they are preventing and will continue to prevent the English from invading the country' and if the fine were to be mitigated, the French would then take the credit.

Sulivan's firmness began to pay off. He had already suggested to the French Admiral that the blockade should be lifted temporarily to allow the foreigners to escape, and the Admiral had objected that the King would be bound to suspect. Now he raised the issue again, this time with the French Captain, de la Taille to whom he said that the lifting of the blockade and subsequent action were imminent, and asked the Frenchman to warn the Europeans, who according to recent information were now enjoying a greater measure of freedom and could therefore concoct means of escape.

The French Captain thanked him for the warning and said he would pass on the message, but deplored the imminent action because new controls had been imposed upon the Europeans for refusing to go to Abomey for the celebrations in honour of the King's mother, and de la Taille also pointed out how difficult it would be for merchants dotted about the country to escape. However, the Frenchman passed on the message and the threat worked, as Sulivan had hoped.

The Avogah (or Governor) wrote to welcome him to a 'palaver,' and apologized for not receiving previous naval officers whom Sulivan had sent ashore with the honour due to them, of which Sulivan had complained, and offered one hundred and fifty puncheons of oil. In reply, Sulivan held out for two hundred, on receipt of which he would raise the blockade. The upshot of this was a meeting between Sulivan and the Avogah to sign the treaty. He had wanted to land with one hundred men as a show of force, but the surf at Whydah was very fierce, and after three surf boats had capsized, he only managed to get ashore after considerable difficulty, accompanied by a handful of officers.

They were met by a large force, and carried in hammocks covered with awnings, in a procession of rudely-armed retainers, drummers and umbrellas bearers across a swamp, and then in canoes over the lagoon to the village of Pacootah, where the Avogah—with a much larger force— awaited their arrival. The Avogah said, with much gesticulation and emphasis, that he had been misrepresented, and 'that nothing was further from the King than the thought of offending Queen Victoria, that King Gelele was very anxious that an English officer should go to Abomey as Ambassador, as he had something particular to say to him, but that now he hoped the blockade would be raised, and that there would be lasting friendship between the English and themselves!' Nevertheless, he continued to be equivocal about the release of the prisoners, and pleaded inability to sign the treaty. Sulivan insisted that until it was returned with the King's assent and the prisoners released, the blockade would not be lifted. At last the Avogah had no alternative but to agree, and the ceremony ended with much shaking of hands and drumming and presentations of bullocks and gems.

Sulivan's trademark can surely be seen in the avuncular tone of the treaty:

> . . . The subjects of Her Britannic Majesty being or residing in the country of Dahomey shall receive special protection from all annoyance and inconvenience in their various occupations or trades from any and all of the subjects of His Majesty Gelele and from foreigners residing in that country ·. . . and the King Gelele engages herewith to issue a proclamation to His Majesty's subjects and to all foreigners in his dominions never again to molest, interfere with, or threaten the lives or persons of British subjects, on pain of severe punishment . . . The export of slaves to foreign countries is for ever abolished in the territories of the King of Dahomey . . . No British subject shall henceforth be compelled to attend any of the customs of the country of Dahomey where any human sacrifices are held . . . Whereas, in consequence of insult and violence towards one of Her Majesty's subjects in the country of Dahomey, a fine has been imposed of 500 puncheons of oil on that kingdom and a blockade established to enforce payment of the same, it is herein agreed, on the part of Her Most Gracious Majesty, that the fine shall be reduced to 400 puncheons of oil and the blockade immediately raised, under the following conditions: that 200 puncheons of oil are paid at once, and the remainder within twelve months from this date; and His Majesty King Gelele agrees to these conditions, and promises herewith to complete the payment of the 400 puncheons of oil by the time given . . .

This was a fitting conclusion to Sulivan's connections with the slave trade, and Commodore Sulivan wrote from Accra on 11 May to say that he had done admirably. 'I congratulate you most heartily on your skill and firmness and hope you will get plenty of credit . . . how glad everyone will be when the blockade is raised.'

CHAPTER 7

LANDFALL

George Sulivan continued to command *Sirius* and took her the following year, 1877, to the West Indies Station where in 1878 he kept a diary recording the more peaceful activities of the New World, although pasted into the flyleaf was a reminder of Africa, a newspaper cutting from the *Globe* referring to the events in Dahomey. The article stated that the King of Dahomey was none the worse for the blockade, that the European firms at Whydah would pay the indemnity, and that the King had even asked Commodore Sulivan for a ship to take his emissaries to England so that the two most powerful monarchs in the world could be on friendly terms. The only gain for the Europeans, who had suffered most from the blockade, was that they would no longer be compelled to attend the ceremony in which slaves were slaughtered.

Also pasted into the front is an epigram by a Mr Cole, the Member of Parliament for Falmouth, who had described the Premier as 'a first-rate courtier, a second rate novelist and a third rate statesman;' but as the back page has a newspaper cutting referring to Benjamin Disraeli as 'the most popular man in Canada, politics out of the question,' we are left in doubt as to Sulivan's political views.

The book itself, Letts Diary and Almanac, is a mine of information: the salaries of the cabinet, the composition of both Houses, the opening times of Madame Tussaud's, how to address nobility and public officers, the Bishops of Scotland, the London banks, tide tables, Anglo-French calculations, colonial mails, abbreviations, instructions for making a Will, all were there. Letts were justly proud of themselves and modestly announced that Dr Livingstone's diary, 'sent home by him per Mr. Stanley' was one of theirs—no. 51 to be precise—'par excellence the best Diary for Travellers use' (cost fourteen shillings). Sulivan was more parsimonious than the Doctor, for his model is no. 12, costing only three shillings. Perhaps with a larger one his writing might have been better, for so much of it is barely decipherable, in contrast to the careful legibility of his ships' logs.

The contents show him in a new light, altogether mellower, enjoying a busy, social life at all his ports of call, with a well developed eye for a pretty face, and there is no hint of his passionate convictions or the single-minded fervour of his loathing of the slave trade.

New Year's day 1878 found *Sirius* three days out of Bermuda bound for Halifax, enduring a 'tremendous gale and terrible sea.' On 3 January, she had to heave to whilst the gale blew from the north-east, and arrived at Halifax the next morning to find the land covered with snow. He drove about the town in a sleigh and dined with a married lady 'and her pretty sister.' A few days later *Sirius* was on her way back steaming across the gulf stream through snow and hail. Back in Bermuda he went to church in the dockyard, the ship was coaled and an engine room artificer was drowned. On the 30th, the Admiral and his lady visited the ship and Bermudans were entertained to an 'at home.' The next day a courtmartial was held on a doctor who was dismissed the ship. No details are given and we are left wondering if the doctor, like the Chaplain of the *London*, had quarrelled with his Captain.

February opened with *Sirius* meeting the fleet, consisting of *Bellerophon*, *Argus* and *Bullfinch*, and sailing to St. Kitts where the onshore squadron beat the St. Kitts squadron at cricket. From there they sailed to St. Johns, Antigua, where Sulivan called on the Governor and went to the cathedral with the Admiral's party. A few days later *Sirius* parted company with the squadron and sailed for English Harbour to take on coals before going on past Martinique, rejoining the squadron at St Vincent where Sulivan lunched with the governor, and then on to Barbados where he paid and returned courtesy calls on the Captains of an Austrian frigate and an American ship.

In March *Sirius* sailed to Port of Spain, Trinidad, Jamaica, Port au Prince and Santo Domingo where a revolution was going on, although the next day the port was surrendered to Government troops. From there, in company with the squadron, *Sirius* sailed to Bermuda where she stayed for several weeks before going to Halifax where she arrived on 24 April. The following Sunday Sulivan went to the Scotch Episcopalian church for both morning and evening services. *Sirius* was only there six days before returning to Bermuda, this time with a lady passenger on board.

In Bermuda they were kept busy, first coaling and then provisioning the ship, and later steaming out of harbour to 'exercise prize firing at targets;' before returning once more to Halifax where there was more coaling to be done during the week, although on Sunday, Sulivan went to the 'Scotch'* church in the morning and (mindful of his mother) the Free Church in the evening. On 24 May, the Queen's birthday, ships were dressed overall, salutes were held, and he attended the governor's ball. The ship was several weeks in Halifax, and weekdays were busy with coaling, provisioning, 'making and straining sails' and the normal routine of shipboard life. The afternoons and evenings saw considerable social activity; an 'at home' was held on board attended by the Admiral and the General commanding the garrison and their ladies, and this entailed a number of drives ashore to return calls and attendance at the Admiral's reception. Sundays were given over mainly to the Scotch church, although Sulivan also went to St Pauls.

On 8 June *Sirius* sailed for Fortune Bay where, after passing between the islands of St Pierre and Macquelon, she anchored three days later. She spent several days on this coast, stopping in small anchorages where Sulivan went ashore and visited fishermen's huts, and at St Jacques harbour he was impressed by the Sabbath calm on Trinity Sunday. Back at St John's the ship was dressed again and a salute of twenty-one guns fired in honour of the anniversary of the Queen's accession to the throne. Two days later the Governor and his wife lunched on board and were saluted

*Sulivan's own usage has been retained.

with seventeen guns on leaving. The following Sunday Sulivan went to the Independent chapel where a Scotch Presbyterian preached and announced plans for the ordination of a Wesleyan minister. The Governor's garden party was cancelled because of the rain, but at a dance which replaced it 'all St. John's turned out, some very nice looking girls amongst them.' The next day the streets were decorated with arches for the reception of the Pope's delegate and Sulivan commented that St John's stank of fish.

The next voyage was to La Scie on the north coast of Newfoundland 'to enquire into outrages on English property by French fishermen,' where Sulivan heard the evidence of witnesses. From there *Sirius* sailed to Canada Bay, where he saw a Carabean (sic) deer on the beach and gave four bibles to 'native' fishermen and women (reminiscent of Bartholomew in the Baltic). On the way from there to Croque harbour, *Sirius* passed fifteen icebergs, although Sulivan only managed to photograph one, presumably his duties on the bridge engaging all his attention. At Croque he went ashore with gun and rod and managed to get a snipe and 'a few' trout, although four other officers caught two hundred between them. After another day's sport, this time plagued by flies and mosquitoes, they sailed for Hare Bay where there was more sport and a conference with a French senior officer about the friction between the fishermen. *Sirius* sailed again, passing more icebergs, which afforded good targets for gunnery practice as well as more opportunities for the Captain to take photographs. At one place ashore they found an old fisherman who 'seemed a Christian man, compared to the majority . . .' who was building a little Wesleyan chapel. The next day he fished a small lake and with some of the crew rowed out to an iceberg, 'a very grand looking thing.'

On the way to Labrador, *Sirius* stopped off one of the capes, and Sulivan sent for the lighthouse keeper in order to give him 'evidence about the wreck of the *Marion*' but learnt that he was in England! At Horne Bay he landed 'in company with a young relative, D. Sullivan,' and the pilot and fished the brook and ponds where he caught forty-one trout.

At Battle harbour he sent a note to Bishop Long whose yacht was at anchor there offering him a tow, which he declined as he was going in the opposite direction to *Sirius* whose next port of call was Dear harbour. There a telegram was received to say that the Congress of Berlin had been 'satisfactorily concluded and Cyprus ceded to England.' It rained incessantly all that day, and the next day there was a 'gale from the North East howling outside.' The following day it had moderated enough for *Sirius* to continue her voyage northwards, passing no less than eighty-one icebergs. At Gready Island Sulivan took two dry plates ashore and obtained two good photographs. As he also saw 'two pretty fisherman's daughters, the first pretty ones I have seen north of St. Johns', the subjects of the photographs remain a matter for conjecture. At Cartwright harbour (on the east coast of Labrador), where it again rained incessantly all day, 'poor old Pilot the dog died' suddenly of heart disease. Sulivan had had him 'since he was a puppy.' Next day a stoker fell overboard from the cutter and was drowned and Sulivan had to make arrangements with the Hudson's Bay Company to locate the body.

The next week was spent cruising off the coast and landing ashore almost daily for shooting and fishing. At St Charles harbour, Sulivan had to hear a complaint about a wreck being plundered and committed the accused for trial although he 'hoped to get them off that.' After reaching Chateau, *Sirius* turned south for Forteau Bay where there was more successful trout fishing, although the salmon were less responsive. From there the voyage was continued southwards to Hawkes Bay and Bonne Bay on the west coast of Newfoundland, where Sulivan was impressed by the 'very picturesque' hinterland and met the clergyman from Bay of Islands whom he heard preach in the local schoolroom. The next day, August Bank Holiday monday, *Sirius* sailed south, towing the mission boat as far as Bay of Islands. From Port-aux-Basques, at the south western tip of Newfoundland, she sailed to Sydney in the north east of Nova Scotia, where she was relieved by another vessel, and after a few days made for Halifax, passing very close to a Cunard steamer in dense fog.

At Halifax, where she found *Bellerophon* and *Argus*, she had to be coaled alongside the jetty and divers had to go down to carry out repairs to her keel, which took several days. On Sunday Sulivan went to the Scotch church and passed much of the following week in social activities. He met the General and several Colonels; and Lady McDougal, Lady Englefield and other local ladies came aboard for 'lunch, tea and dance;' and he went ashore for 'afternoon tea, singing and dancing.'

On 24 August, in company with *Bellerophon* and *Argus*, *Sirius* left Halifax for a courtesy visit to the United States, arriving four days later at Newport, Rhode Island, where salutes were exchanged and the officers attended a reception. The next day there was a lunch on board the flagship attended by the Governor and Mayor and 'thousands of visitors boarded the ships.' Sulivan met a number of American ladies and found the sister of the local congressman's wife to be 'extremely beautiful.' On the 31st he went to a 'hop at Ocean House' (the first appearance of slang in the diary, perhaps under American influence); on Sunday a number of local people attended a service on board *Sirius*, and the next day with 'the elite of Newport Society,' Sulivan attended a real American clambake picnic.

The next evening he embarked on a steamer for a quick visit to New York, arriving the following morning in time for breakfast at the Brunswick Hotel. He then set off sightseeing, a walk that took him up Fifth Avenue and down Sixth Avenue to the elevated railway and back along Broadway. The steamer sailed again in the evening to the accompaniment of much singing and music, and Sulivan likened it to 'a huge hotel.' Back in Newport there was a reception on board *Sirius* and a ball on *Bellerophon*, but on Sunday he went to chapel morning and evening although there was time in between for afternoon tea with a Mrs Perkins. On Monday there was a dinner with the American Commodore and a General, and in the evening a ball at Ocean House was attended by a thousand people. Although the festivities did not end until after three in the morning, the squadron had weighed anchor by eleven o'clock and sailed out of Newport harbour accompanied by a host of sailing craft of all sizes, with people ashore waving from every vantage point.

On the return voyage, *Sirius* underwent full speed trials and back in Halifax moored alongside the careening wharf, where she took on coals. Her Captain had another busy week of engagements in addition to the constant administrative duties on board: on Sunday he went to chapel, on Monday to the Governor's to hear singing and watching the quadrille being practised, and on Wednesday to the gardens to hear the band and to chapel again. On Thursday he gave a dinner party for Mayor Brown and a number of the guests including the flagship's Chaplain (who presumably did not wear ornate vestments), and on Friday a tea party for a Mrs Clark and her niece. Saturday was a day for social calls, and Sunday for church in the morning and Wesleyan chapel in the afternoon.

On Monday, 23 September, in fine weather and a fresh northerly breeze, *Sirius* sailed with *Bellerophon* and *Argus* for Charlottetown, Prince Edward Island, where another round of social duties awaited. He dined with the Governor met congenial people who visited him on board, watched a cricket match in which the Fleet beat the islanders and the officers of the garrison, attended the Governor's reception and for the third time in two days was again with his friends, Chief Justice and Mrs Palmer, whose daughter sang at the Governor's, 'and was evidently the island songstress.' The next day Sulivan 'sang a duet' with her when he returned her family's call, which no doubt put him into an appropriate frame of mind for going on to lunch with the Admiral and a dance that evening on *Bellerophon*. 'The islanders,' he wrote, 'look forward to this annual visit of the Squadron as the great event of the year.' Early the next morning Charlottetown woke to find the ships gone, and its inhabitants returned to their normal preoccupations for another year.

Two days later, the Squadron entered the St Lawrence in fine weather, and steamed up river through 'beautiful country.' That evening they took on the pilot and anchored off Brandy Point, continuing their progress next morning, mooring at Quebec in the evening. The following day the Admiral landed and was saluted by fifteen guns, and Captain Sulivan and the officers of the Squadron attended the Governor's reception. The weekend was very busy with social junketing; he 'went down the river with a large party of ladies and gentlemen and the Governor General, Lord Dufferin, to the Montmorency Falls, landed and lunched there with Miss Griffen and others. . . .' That evening he went to dinner with the Governor General and listed in his diary all the people he met. On Sunday he went to the Scotch church in the morning and the cathedral in the evening; on Monday he lunched with the Admiral and went to a reception on *Bellerophon*; on Tuesday to a cricket match and concert and called on the Chevaliers, whom he had met on the previous day and to whom he had taken a liking (he had taken Miss Chevalier into dinner at the Governor General's) and who came to dinner the next day on board *Sirius*. Unfortunately a gale got up whilst they were dining, a steam cutter sank in the harbour, and he had great difficulty getting his guests ashore between squalls. The next day he went to be photographed 'with D'arcy Irvine and the girls' who he met again that afternoon watching a game of lacrosse and the following day he drove with Irvine to the Montmorency Falls before calling on the Chevaliers who were to leave the next morning for England and Paris.

On 14 October he left by steamer, accompanying Lord Dufferin, to Montreal where he stayed at the Windsor Hotel with the Governor General and his staff. He walked about the town to inspect it and drove up to the top of Green Mountain to see the view, which he found 'very grand,' and the next day he went by train to view the rapids, coming back over them by steamer. He returned by steamer to Quebec for more party-going, and the very next day was breakfasting with the Governor.

Sirius and *Argus* left together for Halifax, but after a few days *Sirius* had to take the other vessel in tow after she had sustained damage in a gale. However, this did not prevent them from exercising at gunnery practice *en route*. Off

Prince Edward Island the ward room officers dined with Sulivan, whose entry for this event is in a shakier hand than any other in the diary. Perhaps his mother's warnings of long ago about 'going beyond the proper bounds' were for once not heeded. On 25 October, with *Argus* still in tow, *Sirius* berthed alongside the wharf at Halifax and began coaling, and on Sunday, as usual, Sulivan attended service ashore. For the next week or so his diary entries were laconic in the extreme: '*Boxer* arrived from the fisheries,' 'dined at the Admiral's,' 'made some calls,' 'Halifax fine weather.' On 7 November he attended a court martial on two men who 'broke out of the ship,' and went to a reception given by the Admiral; a few days later the 101st Regiment arrived from Cyprus to exchange with the 20th, who embarked on the same transport, the *Orontes*. A press cutting, inserted in the diary, reported that they were 'very loath to leave Halifax especially to go to such a frightful place as Cyprus is said to be.' There were a large number of desertions and detachments were ferreting out absentees almost until the moment of departure. As *Orontes* steamed out, the 'yards of the men of war were manned and the blue jackets gave the voyagers three hearty cheers, the band of the 20th and that of *Bellerophon* playing Auld Lang Syne. The Admiralty steamer *Charger* accompanied the troopship down the harbour with a large party of ladies and gentlemen. Numbers crowded on the wharfs and waved handkerchiefs to the departing friends, while wet eyes frequently seen showed that 'fond hearts were left behind . . .' Some of the fond hearts however still had the Squadron to comfort them.

Sulivan was back in his favourite Scotch church on Sunday to hear a Dr Williams preach 'a splendid sermon,' *Sirius* had to leave harbour to look out for a steamer carrying Princess Louise, and passed an uncomfortable four days in gales and a heavy sea until reaching the rendezvous where she failed to connect and had to return to harbour where they caught up with her and Sulivan met the royal passenger at a reception.

After many fond farewells, *Sirius* left Halifax on the last day of November, and after a rough passage in strong north-easterly gales, under storm sails she sailed to Bermuda and went straight into the floating dock. The crew were boarded out to *Irresistible*, and Sulivan had to pay the usual courtesy calls at Government House and Admiralty House; he also went to the dockyard church and for a trip to Hamilton, Clarence Cove,—and 'wrote theatricals' for the 'soldiers' concert' with a number of other ladies and gentlemen—a fascinating entry. He photographed his ship in dock, where she had to remain for nearly a fortnight undergoing essential repairs and overhaul. After a few more days of the social round, *Sirius* left for Jamaica where nine days later, under steam and sail, she sailed slowly through 'lovely country'— past 'the site of the Jamaican mass executions' and on the last day of the year moored alongside the jetty.

The diary gives a picture of Sulivan's lighter moments, but life was not all balls and receptions and the ship's log shows the usual careful entries of life aboard ship, discipline, maintenance and training. The period of the log straddles the time spent both in West African and West Indian waters, and apart from brief references to the blockade of Dahomey there is little difference in the entries. There are the usual meticulous details of wind, weather, course and current; distance, latitude and longitude initialled by officers of the watch; and sails and the times of setting, coals and quantities used; there are exchanges of colours with ships of many nations and welcome contacts with mail ships, but most of the entries concern domestic, nautical and military routine, the latter consisting in entries such as: 'exercised a party at ammunition instruction', 'firing shot and shell at target,' 'read articles of war to ship's company,' 'party of seamen at cutlass drill.' Good seamanship was inculcated by exercising various groups: the ordinary seamen of the watch, the watch aloft, the marines and others. Despite this there were a surprising number of entries for missing articles: a riding cable was carried away and 'lost overboard by fouling,' and entries such as 'broken by accident, boats' mast, one.' A large number of entries are domestic: salutes may be fired, Admirals may visit, officers' dinners and balls held, but the crew continue to be 'employed making and mending clothes,' airing bedding, washing clothes, scrubbing hammocks. Good discipline was maintained, not only on the lower deck and there are several entries such as 'Assistant Paymaster under arrest for returning to duty intoxicated.' On Sundays divine service was 'performed' and often on a weekday prayers were read, and once a month the crew received their 'monthly money.'

Sulivan's diary covered the year 1878, but from the log no inkling could be gained of the busy social life of her Captain in Halifax, Quebec, Newport and elsewhere. Conversely the diary shows nothing of the unending routine of life on a man-of-war. Even at Newport when his shore excursions were most demanding, the 'small arm company' was drilled and the 'backward men' and boys' were exercised at seamanship, and on the day of the Queen's holiday after all the salutes, the crew were employed washing and mending clothes.

Sirius continued to be part of the West Indies Squadron throughout 1879, and although there is no diary to portray the lighter moments, the log continues to afford a picture of naval life in the last quarter of the century.

She spent the first few months in Jamaican waters where she was repainted, and then, between April and June, visited Belize, Port Royal and Port Antoine; the second half of the year she cruised to Colon, Cartagena, Montego Bay, San Domingo and Bermuda. There were several disciplinary incidents that year: a sub-lieutenant was 'reproved and admonished in the presence of the officers' for falling asleep on the floor of the recreation room and for 'sleeping out of the ship without orders;' and in September a Lieutenant was placed under arrest for 'highly disrespectful conduct to the Captain on the quarter deck at grand quarters.' When told off by him (the Captain) with the way he carried out his duties he explained in reply 'oh, all right.' He was released later that evening 'without prejudice to further proceedings,' but no more is heard of the incident. Perhaps tempers were fraying after a long commission in the West Indian waters.

In the new year, 1880, dockyard divers had to place copper on the ship's bottom to repair the ravages of two years at sea and preparations were made for the voyage home. The

Admiral visited the ship, warm clothing was issued, and on 9 January she set out for Halifax, where she stayed for a week and special leave was granted to most of the crew, and on the 17th *Sirius* was at last homeward bound. The weather thickened, the stars could not be observed, and soap and tobacco was issued. On 1 February she was off the Scillies and, at last, on the evening of the 4th, she was made fast to a buoy in Plymouth harbour after saluting the Commander-in-Chief with seventeen guns. The next day the Admiral came aboard, the men were gathered by muster list and exercised at general quarters for him, and in the evening they were employed 'discharging powder and shot.' The next day they moved to Devonport and the crew were given weekend leave, from which they returned to the final stages of the commission, landing spares, 'stripping the ship,' 'getting out guns and gun carriages,' 'getting out chain cables' and returning stores. On Sunday the Roman Catholics and Wesleyans were despatched to their chapels and the Church of England men marched to the dockyard church. On the 25th, the dockyard officers made their inspection, the next day the Royal Marine detachment disembarked and the ship's company were paid off. The last entry in the log reads: 'Sunset. Hauled down the Pendant.'

For the first three months of 1881, George Sulivan was the most senior student attending a course at the Royal Naval College, Greenwich, whose large naval and civilian staff almost exceeded the total number of students. During this period his elder brother, Bartholomew, wrote to say that he would send him an infernal machine, carriage paid, although he could not find the priming tube—which was possibly just as well.

In midsummer, he took over his last command, *Repulse*, an armour plated wooden steam ship of the first reserve, with a complement of three hundred and twenty four men and twenty-four officers. She was commissioned at Portsmouth for the Coastguard service, to be based at Hull, with two tenders and three coastguard 'cruisers' under command. The first few weeks of April were occupied in drawing stores, mustering and paying the new ship's company, bending sails, lighting fires in the boilers, reading the punishment warrant and innumerable other duties. For the first time in any of the logs of ships under Sulivan's command appear entries 'tested electric light,' 'exercised with electric lights.' The yards were manned for a visit by the Queen, the ship's pinnace was pre- pared for duty and in May *Repulse* sailed to Sheerness to fire torpedoes—another novel entry.

From there she sailed to her permanent station at Hull, where the ship was dressed overall for the Queen's birthday and a salute was fired of twenty-one guns. Somehow or other a boat hook was lost overboard, and two hundred and twenty-five pounds of fresh beef were taken aboard, no doubt in readiness for the receipt of drafts of men from the Mablethorpe and Wells divisions.

At the end of the month *Repulse* returned to the Downs and sailed for a summer cruise to Friedrichshafen. Un- fortunately, she went aground but was refloated on the incoming tide in time to join the Squadron at 'steam tactics.' A court of inquiry was held into the grounding, but no one was blamed. At Copenhagen, the king of Denmark went on board *Hercules*, the flag ship, and the crew manned the yards. From there, the *Repulse* sailed to Cronstadt in waters well known to Bartholomew Sulivan, where the Czar of Russia visited them and the yards were manned again. Thence to Kiel, where there were the usual Royal Salutes, although this did not prevent the boys from being exer- cised at seamanship. There were four German Ironclads, and two frigates in Kiel harbour, who accompanied the British Squadron to sea for review by Prince William of Prussia.

Back at Portsmouth there was yet another review, with the Royal Yacht *Victoria and Albert* flying the standards of the Grand Duke of Russia and the Crown Prince of Prussia. The Squadron fired a salute and formed single column of line ahead before the Royal yacht *Alberta* steamed round them with the Queen on board. On 6 August, they dressed the ship for the Duke of Edinburgh's birthday, and then after all these excitements, steamed back to Hull, and entries in the log such as 'lost overboard axes one,' 'employed variously' and 'boys to school.' There were also frequent entries for 'steam up' in the various attached launches and the pinnace, and the usual quarters inspections, gun drill, seamanship, and 'divine services.'

The following summer *Repulse* was again in the south, and on this occasion the Duke of Edinburgh hoisted his flag in *Hercules*. After taking on sixty tons of coal, *Repulse* sailed with the Squadron to Gibraltar where landing parties were exercised. In July she returned to Portsmouth, testing guns and torpedo firing circuits, and in August she was back in Hull, moving between Hull roads, Grimsby and the river Humber, where she stayed through another winter.

The next summer, 1883, she was off again on the annual cruise, this time to Heligoland and Bergen, when the Squadron exercised 'fleet evolutions' and thence to the Shetlands, Lerwick, Invergordon, Cromarty and Leith before once again resuming station in Hull roads.

Sulivan was still commanding in the New Year 1884, but in April a new Captain joined and he relinquished his last command without fanfare or fuss.

The next few years were spent in bachelor retirement, mostly in Cornwall, and he saw a good deal of his brother Bartholomew with whom he was in frequent correspondence. Although their letters are surprisingly formal to modern eyes, ending 'Yours affectionately, B. Sulivan' or G. L. Sulivan, their identity of interest as well as family ties drew them together. Bartholomew wrote to thank George for his photographs and sent him a hooping-cough remedy. George wrote about recognition for his services, Bartholomew referred people to his younger brother's book and described the Golden Jubilee review of the fleet in 1887, which he attended with the Hydrographer, various 'scientific big wigs' including Darwin and his wife, the Astronomer Royal and the President of the Royal Society.

Then, in 1889, three years after his promotion to Rear-Admiral, on the retired list, George Sulivan at the age of fifty-seven, an apparently confirmed bachelor, found himself a wife and went on to have three children.

For some years he had been considering the possibility of

this event, even during his mother's life time, for she had written, in an undated letter:

> You are bound to think of the future interests and happiness of any woman you marry. If the father really desired that his daughter shall have this choice of his property, after his own and her mother's lifes' interests, what could possibly be his objection to securing it to her' She went on to write very knowledgeably of the need for a settlement . . .
> I cannot fancy anyone who cares for his child wishing her future to depend on a mere will which may be altered . . . we have given £1,000 to each child that has married, besides settling an equal share of all after our deaths; and I thought this was all but regular in such cases. I am very sorry for the poor daughter who could know nothing of this; but I am surprised that any father could wish her to be placed in such uncertainty as to her future, when he must know that she could only have a small income from you besides her pension in case of being left a widow.

Despite his mother's unfavourable references, George seems to have been fortunate in having a well-disposed father-in-law, Richard Stirling of Dumbartonshire in Scotland, who wrote, 'Although I might have wished that your means were somewhat greater, I know few of your profession are blessed with riches, and when mutual love and attachment exists it is hoped that much happiness may be in store.'

Fortunately he was right. By all accounts Margaret Hamilton Richie Stirling was an admirable person, eminently suited to coping with a middle-aged bachelor sailor. She only enjoyed fifteen years of married life, and was left to bring up on her own her three children, who held her in great respect as well as affection.

George and Hammie (she was rarely referred to as Margaret) settled in Bournemouth to be near Bartholomew and Sophie who had not long since moved there and were already well known for their good works, their church con-

nections and visits to the poor and the sick. They had survived the tragedy of the early death of their second son,
James, a Lieutenant in the Navy who had died of malarial
fever in South America, and had been buried almost under
the windows of the house in Montevideo where his parents
had endured the siege so many years before. They kept open
house for their many friends of South American days and
naval colleagues who had settled in Bournemouth. The
greenhouse and garden kept them busy, and Bartholomew's
telescope and genial lessons in astronomy were enjoyed by
the young, in particular the daughters of the Bishop of the
Falkland Islands who wrote, after Sulivan's death, that as a
navigator his name 'was a household word in this position of
the southern hemisphere.' He also referred to Bartholomew's great interest in the Tierra del Fuego mission and
his personal qualities: 'the keen intelligence of his face and
the stamp of sincerity upon it, his rich kindly voice and
manners so frank and genial.' . . . He had stood to his
opinions as courageously as he had, as a young man in South
America, stood to his guns. He was the most successful of
the Sulivans and will be remembered wherever the voyage of
Beagle is remembered, and he was the most equable and
good natured of his family. He was a quiet Christian, and
although as highly principled as his younger brother, could
never have been associated with a flamboyant *cause célèbre*
like the Penny affair: nor did he arouse hostility as George
did, nor was he ever an uncomfortable subordinate.

Nevertheless, although Bartholomew devoted time, money
and energy to the South American mission, it was George
who, with all his imperfections, was the crusader and who
continued to interest himself in the suppression of the East
African slave trade, which he had first encountered in the
forties, until his death in the new century.

He and Hammie had been in Bournemouth for less than
two years when Bartholomew died, and only stayed there
until 1892 when, with their two little daughters, Doreen and
Margaret, they moved to 15 Cliveden Place in a sedate area
of well-kept terraced houses near Eaton Square in London.
Hammie enjoyed London life and brought up her daughters

to appreciate its sophistications. She was presented at Court and there were invitations to Buckingham Palace garden parties, to Cowes and to other events of the social season.

Meanwhile, George, who had by now been promoted to Admiral on the retired list, was keeping himself busy with genealogical enquiries. His father, Admiral Thomas Ball Sulivan, had left amongst his papers a roughly sketched family tree showing one Timothy O'Sullivan, son of Daniel O'Sullivan More (Spelt with an 'e'), who had been slain in 1652 defending his castle against a rival who became chief of the family. His son Timothy Cornelius had a son Thomas, who became the father of Timothy, Thomas Ball's father. Before his death Bartholomew had written, in response to his brother's request, to say that when he had been in Cork in 1881 on business for the South American Mission Society, an old lady had said she thought he was probably the O'Sullivan, and recounted a typically involved Irish tale. There had apparently been two families who were great enemies, the O'Sullivans—who were Roman Catholics—and the Sulivans—who were Protestants. The O'Sullivans had three sons, one of whom had two grandsons. One of these had become a Protestant and had been 'turned adrift' by his family and the other had remained a Catholic. The contemporary descendant of one, almost certainly the Protestant, was a Bishop of the Church of Ireland, Dr O'Sulivan, but as the head of the family ought to have been a descendant of the other brother, and as Bartholomew was the oldest grandson of Timothy O'Sullivan, who had been entered for the priesthood before going to sea and therefore could be presumed to represent the Catholic line, the old lady concluded that Bartholomew must be the rightful head of the family. He himself took this with characteristic good humour, writing 'I should adopt her version but as it might not hold water if gone into too closely, I would not dispute the matter . . .' he was personally quite ready 'to allow that Dr. O'Sulivan was the head of the family with all the property, title and advantages. I have never bothered my head about it further.'

Fortunately George did not dispute the title, but he next

PRIMARY SOURCES—AUTOBIOGRAPHY, etc.
G. L. Sulivan, *Dhow Chasing in Zanzibar Waters*, London 1873, reprinted 1967 with an introduction by D. H. Simpson.
J. K. Laughton & J. F. Sulivan, *The Journals of Admiral Bartholomew James*, London 1926.
edited B. J. Sulivan, *The Life & Letters of Admiral Sir Bartholomew James Sulivan*, London 1896.

Letters & Diaries
Letters from Mrs H. Sulivan to her son.
Letters from Admiral Sir Bartholomew Sulivan to his brother.
Diary for 1878 kept by Admiral G. L. Sulivan.
Miscellaneous letters from Admiral G. L. Sulivan and family *bric-à-brac*.

OTHER SOURCES
Hugh P. Oliver, *Notes on the Parish of Mylor*, Taunton 1907; *A Panorama of Falmouth*, Cornish Magazine, Falmouth 1827.
edited J. Betjeman, *Cornwall Illustrated*.
F. Graham, *Cornwall 100 years Ago*, Newton Abbot 1969.

The Navy—general
Carola Oman, *Nelson*, London 1954.
C. Lloyd, *The British Seaman*, London 1968.
M. Lewis, *The History of the British Navy*, London 1957.
M. Lewis, *England's Sea Officers: The Story of the Naval Profession*, London 1948.
M. Lewis, *A Social History of the Navy*, London 1960.
T. D. Manning & C. F. Walker, *British Warship Names*, London 1959.

The Navy—slave trade
C. Lloyd, *The Navy and the Slave Trade*, London 1949.

Coastguard
F. C. Bowen, *H.M. Coastguard*, London 1928.

East Africa—general
R. Coupland, *The Exploitation of East Africa 1856–90*, London 1939.
R. Oliver & G. Mathew, *History of East Africa, Vol. 1* Oxford 1963.

East Africa—Slave trade
P. Collister, *The Last Days of Slavery*, Nairobi 1961.
R. W. Beechey, *The Slave Trade of East Africa*, London 1976.
S. Miers, *Britain and the Ending of the Slave Trade*, London 1975.

West Africa
J. D. Hargreaves, *Prelude to the Partition of West Africa*, London 1966.

The Army—general

The Hon. J. W. Fortescue, *The History of the British Army*, London 1930

D. H. Cole & E. C. Priestley, *An Outline of British Military History*, London 1936.

Kaffir War

R. Godlonton & E. Irving, *A narrative of the Kaffir Wars*, London 1852.

W. R. King, *Campaigning in Kaffir Land,* London 1853.

The Crimean War

P. Gibbs, *Crimean Blunder*, London 1960.

The Abyssinian Campaign

C. Markham, *A History of the Abyssinian Expedition*, London 1896.

Journals, etc.

A Falklands Islands Mystery—Royal Commonwealth Society Library Notes, January 1965.

Czeslaw Jésman, *Theodore II of Ethiopia*, History Today April 1972.

E. A. Gray, *The Stone Frigates of Sevastopol*, History Today June 1969.

INDEX

Ships: List of ships mentioned in text, irrespective of flag

INDEX

ship of that name, 27; Vice-Admiral Norton Allen Sulivan—Bartholomew's grandson—served aboard, 182
Driver: Steamship, 1050 tons. Crimea, 52
Dromedary: Sixth rate: Bartholomew James took command 1797, 5
Dryad: Ethiopian campaign 1860s, 94

Eagle: Seventy-four gun. Built 1804, 82
El Corso: Brig. Bartholomew James temporary command, 5, 6
Exmouth: George Sulivan, 81
Expeditive: French. With combined French and British fleet operations on Coast of Uruguay 1845. Bartholomew Sulivan, 16

Fairy: Royal comings and goings, 81
Fanny: With combined French and British operations on Coast of Uruguay. Bartholomew Sulivan commanding, 1845, 15, 16, 18
Firebrand: Crimean War, 54; With combined French and British Fleet, Coast of Uruguay. Bartholomew Sulivan, 17
Franklin: Captured French ship. Bartholomew James, Post-Captain, 7
Fulton: French. With combined French and British operations, coast of Uruguay. Bartholomew Sulivan, 16, 17; Taken into service in the Crimea. Bartholomew Sulivan, 49
Fury: Crimea, 54

Ganges: Bartholomew Sulivan—operations on Uruguay coast, 13, 15, 17
Gladiator: Spithead, 1867, 91

Golden Fleece: Cargo carrying, Crimean Way, 58
Gorgon: With combined French and British fleet operations on coast of Uruguay 1845, Bartholomew Sulivan, 18
Grinder: Mentioned in Commander Cranford's letter, 74

Hercules: Flagship at Copenhagen, 176; Flagship 'in the south', 177
Highflyer: Slave chasing, 109
Hope: Commanded by Vice-Admiral Norton Allen Sulivan, grandson of Bartholomew Sulivan, 182

Indus: Crew transferred to *Daphne*, 90
Irresistable: Bermuda, 173

Jasper: Gun vessel, Crimean War, 74; Lost during harrassment of Taganrog garrison, 76
June: Crew transferred to *Daphne*, 90

Lightning: Bartholomew Sulivan Survey ship 1854, later served as a fleet tender, 47, 48, 49, 51
Liverpool: Crew transferred to *Daphne*, 90
London: Crimean War, 59, 60; Old wooden two-decker. George Sulivan took command in East African waters, 1874, 143; Extract from Log Book, 146
Lyra: Engaged in capturing slave traders, 128

Magicienne: At Viborg Bay, 62
Maria: Government transport, 1794. Bartholomew James, 3; Barque, 84
Marksman: Commanded by Vice-Admiral Norton Allen Sulivan (Bartholomew Sulivan's grandson), 182

Spartan: 1846. First ship for
George Sulivan, 28

Sphinx: Steam frigate. Crimea, 59

Star: Engaged in harrassment of
slave traders, Zanzibar, 102;
From which George Sulivan
learns of his promotion to
Captain, 1868, 115

Swallow: Crimea, 74

Sweet Poll: Large Causand Bay
boat belonging to Sam, James
and Daniel Sulivan, 11

Syris: P & O Mail Steamer—
George Sulivan sailed in her to
Aden to take over his first
command in *Pantaloon*, 1866,
84

Terrible: Steam frigate, Crimea,
59; Spithead Review, 91

Thetis: Fifth-rate. First appointment Bartholomew Sulivan:
midshipman's training, 12;
Various voyages and engagements, 12, 13

Tiger: Sixteen-gun. Operating
inshore Odessa, 53

Trafalgar: Crimea, 59

Tribune: Balaclava to Yalta.
Crimea, 58, 59

Vengeance: Crimea, 59

Vesuvius: George Sulivan's ship at
Odessa. Crimea, 53, 54, 55, 56,
58, 59, 61; Kertch expedition,
Crimea, 72; Extracts from log,
1855, 78, 79

Victoria & Albert: Royal Steam
Yacht. George Sulivan
appointed Mate and joined crew
in January 1853, 45; After
Crimea, George Sulivan returned to *Victoria & Albert* and
was promoted Commander, 1862,
81; Portsmouth Review, 176

Victory: Bartholomew James
joined as Lieutenant in 1796 for
blockade Toulon, 4; Later
promoted Master. Muster Book
for 16 October 1805, 4

Ville de Paris: Flag ship of Vice-
Admiral Hamelin, Crimea, 60

Vulture: Crimea, 63; With
Daphne and *Briton*, blockade
coast to north of Zanzibar,
1874, 142

Warrior: Iron ship, 1860, 27

Woolwich: Commanded by
Thomas Ball Sulivan, 10

Wrangler: Crimea, 75

Daniel O'Sullivan
m. Helena Macaulffe
d. 1652

John O'Sullivan of Drominagh
m. Mary O'Keefe
d. 1652

Timothy O'Sullivan of Clonfert
b. 1652
m. Joan O'Callaghan
d. 1706

Philip
O'Sullivan
b. 1682
d. 1737

Rear Admiral Bartholemew James
b. at Falmouth 28.12.1752
m. Henrietta Pender
d. 1828

Rear Admiral Thomas Ball Sulivan CB
b. at Cawsand 5.1.1781
m. 19.3.1808 Henrietta Pender, d. of
Rear Admiral Bartholemew James and
Henrietta Pender
d. 16.11.1857

Lt Sam Hood Sulivan RN
b. 1789
d. 1836

James Sulivan:

Lt James Inglefield Sulivan RN
b. 1792
d. 1831

Commander William C. Sulivan RN
d. 1894

Admiral Sir Batholemew
James Sulivan KCB
b. at Mylor 18.11.1810
m. 1837 Sophia, d. of
Admiral James Young and
Charlotte Fyers
d. 1.1.1890

Lt Norton
Sulivan RN
b. 1820·
m. Christine Frase
d. 1850

Cmdr Thomas Digby
Sulivan RN
b. 1823
m. Philomena d. of
General Wolrige
d. 1876

Admiral George Lydiard
Sulivan
b. at Mylor March 1832
m. 1889 Margaret
Hamilton Ritchie d. of
Richard Stirling
d. 3.7.1904

Cmdr James Young
Sulivan RN
b. Falkland Islands
16.3.1844
m. Eleanor Evelyn
Light d. of William
Edward Light
d. 1902

Lt Thomas
Sulivan RN
b. 25.1.1846
d. 5.1.1873

Henry Norton
Sulivan
b. 21.5.1849
m. 9.4.1875
d. 1942

Malcolm
Sulivan
b.1863

Ambrose
Sulivan
b. 1868

Philip
Sulivan
b. 1874

Frances
Sulivan
b. 1862
d. 26.11.1956

Cdr George
Hamilton
Stirling
Sulivan RN
d. 1961

Thomas Light Sulivan
b. 13.10.1883
m. Winifred Aylwin Foster
d. 4.5.1965

Vice Admiral Norton Allan Sulivan CVO
b. 28.1.1879
m. 1912 Gladys Eva, d. of Leonard
James Maton
d. 30.9.1964

Barbara Aylwin
Sulivan
b. 1914
m. Brigadier
Alan Martin
Jenkins CBE

Diana Dorothy
Sulivan
b. 1916
m. Peter
Parkhouse
m. Capt Nigel
Clogstown-
Willmott DSO DSC RN

Col John
Antony Sulivan
b. 1916
m. Elizabeth
Stevens

Moira Sulivan
b. 1913

Grace Joan
Sulivan
b. 1918
m. Rear Admiral
James Harkness
CB

Major Timothy
John Sulivan RA
b. 1946
m. Jane Ellwood

Anthony Marcus
Sulivan
b. 1953

THE SULIVAN FAMILY

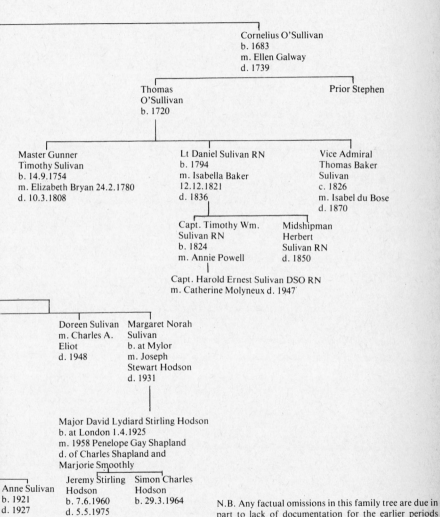

Cornelius O'Sullivan
b. 1683
m. Ellen Galway
d. 1739

Thomas
O'Sullivan
b. 1720

Prior Stephen

Master Gunner
Timothy Sulivan
b. 14.9.1754
m. Elizabeth Bryan 24.2.1780
d. 10.3.1808

Lt Daniel Sulivan RN
b. 1794
m. Isabella Baker
12.12.1821
d. 1836

Vice Admiral
Thomas Baker
Sulivan
c. 1826
m. Isabel du Bose
d. 1870

Capt. Timothy Wm.
Sulivan RN
b. 1824
m. Annie Powell

Midshipman
Herbert
Sulivan RN
d. 1850

Capt. Harold Ernest Sulivan DSO RN
m. Catherine Molyneux d. 1947

Doreen Sulivan
m. Charles A.
Eliot
d. 1948

Margaret Norah
Sulivan
b. at Mylor
m. Joseph
Stewart Hodson
d. 1931

Major David Lydiard Stirling Hodson
b. at London 1.4.1925
m. 1958 Penelope Gay Shapland
d. of Charles Shapland and
Marjorie Smoothly

Anne Sulivan
b. 1921
d. 1927

Jeremy Stirling
Hodson
b. 7.6.1960
d. 5.5.1975

Simon Charles
Hodson
b. 29.3.1964

N.B. Any factual omissions in this family tree are due in part to lack of documentation for the earlier periods and the need to respect the privacy of living members and their families. Only those details concerning 20th century family members which have been voluntarily furnished by themselves or relatives have been included. The object of the Tree is not to convey minutiae of the immediate past but to demonstrate the long seafaring connection and the place of Admiral Sir Bartholomew Sulivan and more particularly his brother Admiral George Sulivan in the line of descent.